W9-DIP-028

Assessing Site Significance

HERITAGE RESOURCES MANAGEMENT Series
Series Editor: DON FOWLER, *University of Nevada, Reno*

Sponsored by the Heritage Resources Management Program, Division of Continuing Education, University of Nevada, Reno

Books in this series are concise, practical guides designed to help those who work in cultural resources management, environmental management, heritage preservation, and related subjects. Based on the successful workshops sponsored by University of Nevada, Reno, the books are designed to be "workshops between book covers" on important strategic, legal, and practical issues faced by those who work in this field. Books are replete with examples, checklists, worksheets, and worldly advice offered by experienced practitioners in the field.

Volumes in this series:

1. CULTURAL RESOURCE LAWS AND PRACTICE: An Introductory Guide, Thomas F. King
2. FEDERAL PLANNING AND HISTORIC PLACES: The Section 106 Process, Thomas F. King
3. ASSESSING SITE SIGNIFICANCE: A Guide for Archaeologists and Historians, Donald L. Hardesty and Barbara J. Little

Assessing Site Significance

A Guide for Archaeologists and Historians

Donald L. Hardesty
Barbara J. Little

ALTAMIRA
PRESS

A Division of Rowman & Littlefield Publishers, Inc.
Walnut Creek • Lanham • New York • Oxford

ALTAMIRA PRESS
A Division of Rowman & Littlefield Publishers, Inc.
1630 North Main Street, #367
Walnut Creek, CA 94596
http://www.altamirapress.com

Rowman & Littlefield Publishers, Inc.
4720 Boston Way
Lanham, MD 20706

12 Hid's Copse Road
Cumnor Hill, Oxford OX2 9JJ, England

British Library Cataloguing in Publication Information Available

Library of Congress Cataloging-in-Publication Data
Hardesty, Donald L., 1941–
    Assesssing site significance : a guide for archaeologists and historians / Donald L.
    Hardesty and Barabara J. Little.
        p. cm.—(Heritage resources management series ; v. 3)
        Includes bibliographical references (p.) and index.
        ISBN 0-7425-0315-1 (cloth : alk. paper)—ISBN 0-7425-0316-X (pbk. : alk. paper)
        1. Historic sites—United States—Management. 2. United States—Antiquities. 3.
    Archaeology and history—United States. 4. Archaeology—Methodology. 5.
    Excavations (Archaeology)—United States. I. Little, Barbara J. II. Title. III. Series.

E159.H26 2000
930.1'028—dc21   00-042004

Printed in the United States of America

♾™ The paper used in this publication meets the minimum requirements of American
National Standard for Information Sciences—Permanence of Paper for Printed Library
Materials, ANSI/NISO Z39.48–1992.

Contents

Information Needs Focus, 157
Abundant Sites Are Significant, 157
Recent Sites Are Not Isolated, 158

Foreword

A key word in the complex federal preservation system, built upon the National Historic Preservation Act, its regulations, and various other related laws and regulations, is *significance*. Persons involved in the cultural side of heritage resources management must wrestle with the issue of whether or not a cultural property or object (such as a historic ship) is eligible for inclusion in the National Register of Historic Places. The authors tell us that to be listed, or to be eligible to be listed, such "historic properties" must be "considered significant to the archaeological, historic, architectural, engineering or cultural heritage of the United States."

The relevant regulations provide a list of significance criteria. Even though the list is rather long, it cannot cover every eventuality and hence, significance is subject to interpretation. The authors of this volume draw upon their extensive knowledge and working experience in providing an excellent guide to assessing and establishing the significance of historic archaeological sites and, hence, eligibility determinations for listing in the National Register.

The authors bring complementary skills to the volume. Don Hardesty has some three decades of experience in historic archaeology and is an internationally recognized authority on the archaeology of historic mines and mining towns. Barbara Little has worked extensively in historic archaeology and was for four years on the staff of the National Register of Historic Places before moving to the Archeology and Ethnography Division of the National Park Service. Both have spent much time and effort assessing and determining significance and they share their knowledge and insights in the present work. The volume is a most worthy addition to our series, building on and complementing two previous volumes by Tom King, which provide general descriptions and discussions of the preservation system and how it operates. We are pleased to be able to present it to the heritage preservation management community and others concerned with cultural heritage in the country.

Don Fowler, Director
Heritage Resources Management Program,
University of Nevada, Reno
March 10, 2000

Preface

Assessing the significance of archaeological remains is one of the most difficult procedures in cultural resource management. That very old and unique archaeological sites are important seems obvious to most people, but what about more recent and very common sites? The archaeological remains of the last five hundred years, that period of time often called the modern world, are difficult to assess for this very reason. They often are not particularly rare and certainly are not old by archaeological standards. Nineteenth-century farmstead sites in the eastern United States are a good example. Yet they often make up a large part of the cultural resources that must be managed. In a general sense, this book, which focuses on how to assess the significance of the archaeological remains of the modern world, grew out of that need. More specifically, the book emerged from several professional training workshops on the topic in which both of us participated, sponsored by the Heritage Management Program at the University of Nevada, Reno (UNR). We thank the workshop participants for their valuable comments. We also thank Don Fowler, director of the Heritage Resources Management Program at UNR, and Mitch Allen of AltaMira Press for their help in initiating this book and bringing it to completion. Barbara Little also would like to thank her coworkers at the National Register of Historic Places for their day-to-day collegiality.

PART ONE

APPROACHES TO ASSESSING SIGNIFICANCE

1

Introduction

In the United States, cultural resource managers face some of their most challenging problems in the archaeological remains of the last five hundred years, a period of time often called the modern world. Perceptions of the value of sites appear to be tied to age, relative abundance, and association with particular themes. The more recent the remains, the more confusion there is about the value of the property. Few managers would argue that the sites of early contact between native peoples and invading Europeans are unimportant. Few fail to see a value in fortifications or battlefields. Far more would disagree that twentieth-century sites are likely to yield important information.

Generally, recent sites are the most abundant of all sites and, therefore, are the most likely to be encountered during a field survey. Their very abundance, however, raises a plethora of questions about archaeological significance. Why, for example, if hundreds or even thousands of examples already exist in site files, is yet another example important? Furthermore, modern world sites have often been documented by abundant written records and oral testimony of people who once lived at the sites. Why should their archaeological remains be important? What additional information could they possibly provide? Sites occupied by European Americans are particularly subject to this skepticism because of the widespread belief that documentary history records nearly everything of importance. The argument is frequently made that recent archaeological sites are significant only if they represent some event that lacks historical documentation. Finally, modern world sites typically are too close

3

to us in time to be seriously considered historic and, therefore, worthy of special consideration. Why, for example, should twentieth-century sites be considered significant? This book discusses the procedures for and issues underlying the evaluation of the archaeological significance of modern world sites, with particular attention given to properties of the industrial age.

WHAT IS THE MODERN WORLD?

The modern world is both a time period and a social and cultural pattern or type marked by large-scale social systems operating within world economies. Some trace the beginning of the modern world to the emergence of a capitalistic world economy in western Europe during the long sixteenth century, beginning about A.D. 1450 (Wallerstein 1974). Others trace its origins to an earlier or later time and to different places (e.g., Abu-Lughod 1989, Frank and Gills 1993, Sanderson and Hall 1995, Wolf 1982). Whatever its time and place of origin, however, the changes that marked the modern world social and cultural pattern clearly intensified in the last five hundred years. The modern world of the last five hundred years is an age of nation-states and other large-scale social systems. They are based on a variety of local and regional modes of production linked together by asymmetrical relations of exchange of goods and services and operating within capitalistic world economies. The modern world is differentiated into regions where wealth and power accumulate. It also is an age of global population movements, conflict, social and cultural diversification, urbanization, industrialization, and environmental change. During approximately the last two hundred years, the modern world has been involved in the industrial age.

MODERN WORLD ARCHAEOLOGICAL REMAINS

Historical archaeology studies the archaeological remains that document and symbolize the social and cultural pattern of the modern world. The remains range from isolated artifacts to townsites and regional landscapes. They include the archaeological record of domestic households, neighborhoods, local settlements, and regional communities, and they include industrial sites, military sites, burial sites, underwater sites, and a great variety of special purpose and multiple purpose sites (Orser and Fagan 1995). Modern world remains include sites occupied by European, African, and Asian Americans as well as native peoples.

Several site types illustrate the modern world particularly well. Global population movements, which brought conflicts, encounters, and episodes of rapid social and cultural change, are one hallmark of the modern world. Conflict-related sites include military encampments, fortifications, and battlefields. The archaeological expression of global population movements also includes remains of migrant farmsteads and villages, Indian reservations, ethnic architecture and landscapes, exploration camps and landmarks, overland emigration trails and camps, and transportation networks and facilities (e.g., railroads, canals, riverboats and steamships, sailing ships and ocean liners, ferries and landings, overland toll roads for stages and freight wagons, automobile highways, and airports).

Another hallmark of the modern world is commerce and industry. Commercial sites include stores, ports of trade, and warehouses. The archaeological record of modern world industry includes the remains of

- extraction or mining activities (e.g., base and precious metals, coal, petroleum, rock and mineral quarries, lumbering);
- manufacturing and factory-related activities (e.g., textile mills, potteries, glass works, firearms factories);
- large-scale agriculture (e.g., plantations, irrigation farming, ranching); and
- power and utilities (e.g., electrical power plants and transmission networks, windmills, water wheels, gas and sewer systems, steam works, telegraph and telephone systems).

THE VALUE OF MODERN WORLD SITES

Cultural resource managers face the enormous problem of assigning a value to archaeological remains. Several years ago William

Lipe (1984) argued that archaeological sites and cultural resources in general have four values embedded in their social and cultural context. First of all, they may have economic value as commodities, especially as tourist attractions or for adaptive reuse. Second, cultural resources might gain value from their association with, or as symbols of, important historical events, themes, and patterns or from their association with important architectural styles or engineering types. In this way, they also could have symbolic value acquired from their meaning within a specific social and cultural context. Traditional cultural properties, for example, symbolize the traditions of ethnic groups. Third, cultural resources could have information value as a repository of data important to scientific or scholarly research. Finally, cultural resources might have aesthetic values, for example, pleasing architectural styles or landscapes.

Associated with the importance of archaeological sites is the value we place on them through the ways we commemorate them. A few are interpreted directly to the visiting public; some are featured on Internet sites; some are listed in the National Register of Historic Places. However, only about 7 percent of the properties listed in the National Register, the official list of the nation's cultural resources considered worthy of preservation, are archaeological. Many archaeologists believe that there is no real point in going to the trouble of nominating a site or district, because under Section 106 of the National Historic Preservation Act, the same protection is afforded a site determined eligible for listing as one that is actually listed. However, listing in the National Register serves to authenticate the worth of a historic place and influences a community's attitude toward its heritage. The National Register plays an important role in influencing both public perceptions and policy decisions about what is significant in U.S. history (see, e.g., Little 1999).

What about the archaeological value of modern world sites? Most of us would not question the importance of the oldest and rarest of the archaeological remains of the modern world. Who would deny that the site of the first English settlement in Virginia at Jamestown is important? Or the Little Bighorn battlefield in Montana? These cultural resources clearly have important economic, associative, information, and even aesthetic values. But what about more recent and more abundant sites? Their very abundance and youth would seem to deny them at least economic and associative value and place into question their information value. The information value of modern world sites appears to be jeopardized especially by the existence of documents and oral testimony that can be used as sources of information that are independent of the archaeological record. The material remains of the modern world, unlike most remains of the more remote past, clearly do not exist in a vacuum. The most fundamental issue in evaluating the archaeological significance of modern world sites, therefore, might be the relative importance of documents, oral testimony, and the archaeological record in understanding or interpreting the past. To what extent does the archaeological record merely duplicate information available from other sources of information, such as written accounts?

The issue of information redundancy is discussed in more detail in chapter 3. In some ways, the issue is one of proportionality. Assuming that all sites contain some useful information or symbolize something of historical importance, are they all significant enough to be given special treatment such as listing on the National Register of Historic Places (NRHP)? On the other hand, should all young sites—those less than one hundred years old—or all abundant site types be summarily dismissed as having no recognizable historic value?

In addition, the localization of cultural resource values must be taken into account in assessing significance. What some may view as ugly scars on the landscape or poisonous waste left behind by past mining activities, for example, may symbolize a glorious past to local residents.

THE LEGAL CONTEXT OF SIGNIFICANCE

Managing the cultural resources of the modern world takes place within many arenas, frameworks, or contexts. The cornerstone of cultural resource management, however, lies in a complex of government laws, policies, and implementing regulations. Thomas King (1998) provides a complete overview. Links to laws, regulations, standards, and conventions can be found on the Internet at http://www.cr.nps.gov/linklaws.htm. Federal legislation regulating cultural resources in the United States began with the Antiquities Act of 1906. Table 1.1 shows the most important subsequent legislation. Of these, the National Historic Preservation Act (NHPA) of 1966, which requires that all federal agencies consider the impacts of undertakings (agency activities and authorizations) on cultural resources, established the current regulatory framework. Later amendments to the 1966 NHPA further require that:

- federal agencies inventory, evaluate, and nominate to the NRHP all significant cultural resources under their jurisdiction;
- effects upon significant cultural resources must be evaluated and the Advisory Council on Historic Preservation must be allowed to comment before agency projects can begin;
- adverse effects upon significant cultural resources must be mitigated.

The Department of the Interior, the agency in charge of implementing the NHPA, issued several key regulations to implement the cultural resource laws (table 1.2). Table 1.3 shows the key documents containing the guidelines for working within the regulations. The NHPA of 1966 established the NRHP to recognize nationally important cultural resources.

The next chapter describes the process of evaluating the eligibility of the archaeological remains of historical sites for the NRHP.

Table 1.1   Key Cultural Resources Legislation

Antiquities Act of 1906
Historic Sites Act of 1935
National Historic Preservation Act of 1966, as Amended
National Environmental Policy Act of 1969
Archaeological and Historic Preservation Act of 1974
Archaeological Resources Protection Act of 1979
Abandoned Shipwreck Act of 1987
Native American Graves Protection and Repatriation Act
Section 303 of the Amended Department of Transportation Act

Table 1.2 Key Cultural Resources Regulations

36 CFR Part 60	National Register of Historic Places
36 CFR Part 61	Procedures for State, Tribal, and Local government historic preservation programs
36 CFR Part 63	Determination of eligibility for inclusion in the National Register of Historic Places
36 CFR Part 68	The Secretary of Interior's Standards for Historic Preservation Projects
36 CFR Part 73	World Heritage Convention
36 CFR Part 78	Waiver of Federal agency responsibility under section 110 of the National Historic Preservation Act
36 CFR Part 800	Protection of Historic Properties (Advisory Council on Historic Preservation). Revised Section 106 regulations took effect on June 17, 1999.

The following regulation governs National Historic Landmarks:

36 CFR 65	National Historic Landmarks Program

The following regulations govern the Federal Archeology Program:

43 CFR Part 3	Preservation of American Antiquities
43 CFR Part 7	Protection of Archeological Resources
43 CFR Part 10	Native American Graves Protection and Repatriation Act
36 CFR Part 79	Curation of Federally Owned and Administered Archeological Collections

Table 1.3 Cultural Resources Guidelines

Archeology and historic preservation: Secretary of the Interior's Standards and Guidelines (Federal Register 48:190, September 29, 1983)
Guidelines for Federal Agency Responsibilities, under Section 110 of the National Historic Preservation Act
Abandoned Shipwreck Guidelines
National Register Bulletins (http://www.cr.nps.gov/nr/nrpubs.html).

2

Determining National Register Eligibility

The National Register of Historic Places (NRHP) is the key to cultural resources evaluation within the U.S. federal regulatory framework. Established by the NHPA, the NRHP lists historic properties that are considered to be significant to the archaeological, historic, architectural, engineering, or cultural heritage of the United States. Historic properties are defined in the NHPA as any "district, site, building, structure, or object included in or eligible for inclusion in the National Register, including artifacts, records, and material remains related to such a property or resource." Districts are geographically grouped objects, buildings, structures, or sites that together are considered to be significant (36 CFR [Code of Federal Regulations] 60). Districts also may be "landscapes that have been shaped by historical (and cultural) processes of land use and retain visual and cultural characteristics indicative of such processes" (Derry et al. 1985: 11). Regulations found in 36 CFR 60 list the criteria, integrity, levels of significance, age, and exceptions that must be used to evaluate and nominate properties to the NRHP. Guidance is issued by the National Register in its series of bulletins (found at www.cr.nps.gov/nr/). Regulations in 36 CFR 63 and 36 CFR 800 detail the process for determinations of eligibility. Five general steps in evaluating the eligibility of archaeological properties under the National Register criteria are shown in table 2.1.

Table 2.1   General Steps for Evaluating the Eligibility of Properties

Eligibility Step 1.	Categorize the property.
Eligibility Step 2.	Determine which historic context(s) the property represents and how property types relate to the archaeological resources.
Eligibility Step 3.	Evaluate significance under National Register criteria A–D.
Eligibility Step 4.	Apply criteria considerations.
Eligibility Step 5.	Determine if property retains sufficient integrity to convey its significance.

ELIGIBILITY STEP 1: CATEGORIZE THE PROPERTY

In practice, the first two steps shown in table 2.1 are quite closely linked, as property types and the categories into which they fit are anticipated and documented within a historic context. All listed properties are classified according to these categories: objects, buildings, structures, sites, and districts. An object is a small-scale or artistic property, such as a monument or mile marker. A building is a property used as shelter for human activity, such as a house or factory. A structure is a property used for human activity that is not a shelter, such as bridge or roadway. A site is a location with significance, such as an archaeological site or a garden. A district is a significant concentration, linkage, or continuity of sites, buildings, or objects united historically or aesthetically by plan or physical development, such as a rural village or a canal system. A property comprises a single entry in the National Register but may consist of more than one physical entity. An archaeological district, for example, may contain several or even hundreds of individual sites but would still be counted as one property listed on the National Register. The categories of property are not the same as property types. For example, a historic context for colonial farmsteads may list several different types of outbuildings as specific property types, but each of these would fall under the category building in the National Register database.

Districts are made up of more than one resource, each of which must be counted as contributing or noncontributing. An archaeological resource is contributing if it independently meets National Register criteria, if it was present during the period of significance, if it relates to the significance of the property, if it retains integrity reflecting its character at the time, or if it has good information value. A resource is noncontributing to a district if it does not independently meet National Register criteria, or if it was not present during the period of significance, or if it does not relate to the significance of the property, or if it does not retain integrity reflecting its character at the time, or if it does not have information value. A noncontributing resource is not necessarily ineligible for the National Register. For example, in a district composed of numerous archeological sites and some standing structures in a townsite with a period of significance from 1835 to 1860, prehistoric sites that fall within the boundary would be noncontributing to that district. They may well be eligible individually, but they are noncontributing to the historic significance of that property as it has been defined.

ELIGIBILITY STEP 2: DETERMINE WHICH HISTORIC CONTEXT(S) THE PROPERTY REPRESENTS AND HOW PROPERTY TYPES RELATE TO THE ARCHAEOLOGICAL RESOURCES

A historic context may be defined as "a broad pattern of historical development . . . that may be represented by historic resources" (Derry et al. 1985: 14). For an archaeological property evaluated for its information value, the historic context is the analytic framework within which the property's importance can be understood. Establishing historic contexts involves identifying important historical patterns through the review of known history. Historic contexts are refined as new information and new resources are discovered. Decisions regarding the evaluation of properties require placing the property in historic context. Therefore, the more that is known about a given context, the better will be the evaluation decisions made about particular properties. One decides whether a property is significant within its historic context(s) by addressing:

- what facet of history the property represents in local, state, or national context;
- how that facet of history is significant;
- if the property type is relevant and important in illustrating the context(s); and
- how this particular property illustrates that facet of history.

The level of context of archaeological sites significant for their information value depends on the scope of the applicable research design. A property with national significance helps us to understand the history of the nation. It must be of exceptional value in representing or illustrating an important theme in national history.

The concept of historic context has two meanings. First, a historic context can be understood as an organizing structure for interpreting history that groups information about historic properties that share a common theme, place, and time. Second, a historic context can be interpreted as those patterns or trends by which a specific occurrence, property, or site is understood and its meaning within prehistory or history is made clear.

There are four general steps to creating historic contexts. These steps are shown in table 2.2.

Context Step 1: Identify the Theme, Time Period, and Geographic Limits

The dimensions of time, place, and theme define all historic contexts. Approaches to the development of specific historic contexts, however, may focus on any one of the dimensions. Chronology, for example, may be the key to interpreting the importance of a partic-

Table 2.2   General Steps in Creating a Historic Context

Context Step 1.	Identify the theme, time period, and geographic limits.
Context Step 2.	Assemble existing information and synthesize the information.
Context Step 3.	Define property types.
Context Step 4.	Identify further information needs.

ular property. The historic context defines the "period of significance" for the property. The historic context also defines the boundaries of the geographical area associated with the property. Place,
however, means many different things for purposes of developing
historic contexts and may include political subdivisions, topo-
graphic or ecological subdivisions, land management units, or culturally meaningful spatial units. The relationship among place, National Register concepts, and archaeological resources can be
complicated. Consider, for example, historic mining districts as the
key dimension of place of a historic context. After the discovery of
an ore body, miners organized themselves into districts, legal enti-
ties recognized by custom and statute, to regulate mining activities
and resolve disputes. They often defined the district's boundaries
arbitrarily rather than precisely encompassing the ore body. A mining district meets the requirements of a historic district. A historic
district is defined as "a significant concentration, linkage, or continuity of sites, buildings, structures, or objects united historically or
aesthetically by plan or physical development" (National Park Service [NPS] 1991a, see also Noble and Spude 1992: 19). In addition,
the properties making up historic districts should not be in different places; however, if the historic properties are geographically
separated but are still unified by a common theme, the district can
be defined with discontiguous boundaries. Historic mining districts
are organized around and related to the extraction and beneficiation of geographically distinct ore bodies. Many historic mining
districts also form a coherent rural historic landscape created by
mining-related land use practices (Noble and Spude 1992: 13–14).
As a historic district, the Bullfrog mining district in southwestern
Nevada contains sites, buildings, structures, and objects that may
or may not contribute to its historic significance. Contributing properties convey the significant time period, place, and themes of the
historic context; noncontributing properties do not. The historic
context, finally, defines the thematic framework within which the
property is to be interpreted or understood. Theme-based historic
contexts, furthermore, encompass a variety of approaches. They
may be organized, for example, around a particular historical event
or pattern such as the Civil War, a scientific or scholarly explanatory framework such as evolutionary theory, a set of cultural values

such as Mormon or Paiute culture, or a resource management strategy such as ecosystem management.

Context Step 2: Assemble Existing Information and Synthesize the Information

Using the NPS Thematic Framework

The National Park Service recently revised its thematic framework for history and prehistory to reflect current scholarship and represent the full diversity of America's past. The thematic framework is used as a tool for analyzing knowledge about historic resources and for developing more complete (or holistic) stories about a particular place. The new framework is broad and is meant to encourage integration of topics and inclusive historic contexts. The *Revised Thematic Framework* (NPS 1996) provides guidance on the development of historic contexts. Consideration of its main themes and associated topics will promote historic contexts that are inclusive of many levels of community and regional as well as national history. The revised framework includes eight major themes for developing historic contexts. Each of the national themes encompasses several subthemes or topics. The full text of the thematic framework may be found at www.cr.nps.gov/history/thematic.html. Figure 2.1 schematically illustrates the intent of the framework. Table 2.3 shows the themes and topics.

In her *Draft Historic Context on Labor Archaeology,* Theresa Solury (1999) uses the NPS thematic framework to organize issues relating to workers' housing and communities. Within the theme "Peopling Places" she considers how industry's demands for a labor force and the location of raw materials such as ore deposits influence population movements into previously isolated regions. The archaeological remains of labor camps evolving into permanent settlements would provide good illustrations of this theme. It may be more difficult to illustrate the theme "Creating Social Institutions and Movements" with archaeological properties. However, there may be remains associated with workers' mutual aid societies or recreational activities such as factory baseball leagues.

"Expressing Cultural Values" is a broad theme. The topic of popular and traditional culture would be one of the most relevant to archaeology. For an archaeology of labor, the topics under

Figure 2.1   National Park Service Thematic Framework

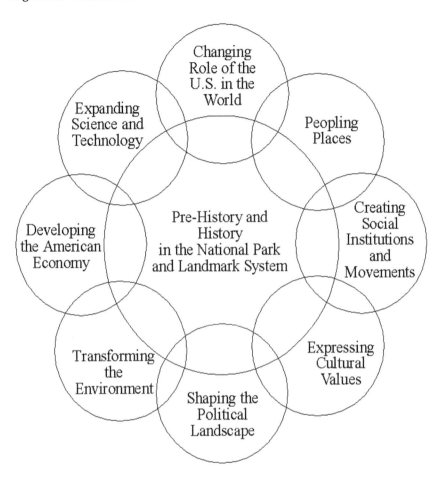

www.cr.nps.gov/history/thematic.html

Developing the American Economy. Includes eight topics: extraction and production, distribution and consumption, transportation and communication, workers and work cultures, labor organizations and protests, exchange and trade, governmental policies and practices, and economic theory.

Table 2.3   Themes and Topics of the National Park Service's Thematic Framework

  I. PEOPLING PLACES
      1. Family and the life cycle
      2. Health, nutrition, and disease
      3. Migration from outside and within
      4. Community and neighborhood
      5. Ethnic homelands
      6. Encounters, conflicts, and colonization

 II. CREATING SOCIAL INSTITUTIONS AND MOVEMENTS
      1. Clubs and organizations
      2. Reform movements
      3. Religious institutions
      4. Recreational activities

III. EXPRESSING CULTURAL VALUES
      1. Educational and intellectual currents
      2. Visual and performing arts
      3. Literature
      4. Mass media
      5. Architecture, landscape architecture, and urban design
      6. Popular and traditional culture

 IV. SHAPING THE POLITICAL LANDSCAPE
      1. Parties, protests, and movements
      2. Governmental institutions
      3. Military institutions and activities
      4. Political ideas, cultures, and theories

"Shaping the Political Landscape" are not easily addressed. The introduction of unions and various armed conflicts between unionized labor and management, however, may provide important insights into the political conflicts of the industrial age. Most of the topics under "Developing the American Economy," particularly that of "workers and work culture," are obviously relevant to an archaeology of labor. Research into workers' communities sheds light on differential conditions within a company town, for example, for owners, foreman, and workers of various nationalities. The effects of consumer products and factory discipline on domestic life may be revealed in the archaeological record. Because industrialization was fueled by technological changes, several topics under the theme "Expanding Science and Technology" can be investigated ar-

V. DEVELOPING THE AMERICAN ECONOMY
  1. Extraction and production
  2. Distribution and consumption
  3. Transportation and communication
  4. Workers and work culture
  5. Labor organizations and protests
  6. Exchange and trade
  7. Governmental policies and practices
  8. Economic theory

VI. EXPANDING SCIENCE AND TECHNOLOGY
  1. Experimentation and invention
  2. Technological applications
  3. Scientific thought and theory
  4. Effects on lifestyle and health

VII. TRANSFORMING THE ENVIRONMENT
  1. Manipulating the environment and its resources
  2. Adverse consequences and stresses on the environment
  3. Protecting and preserving the environment

VIII. CHANGING ROLE OF THE UNITED STATES IN THE WORLD COMMUNITY
  1. International relations
  2. Commerce
  3. Expansionism and imperialism
  4. Immigration and emigration policies

chaeologically. Analysis of privy contents for parasites and dietary clues, for example, reveals information on the changing diet of workers. Particularly in the industrial age, "Transforming the Environment" is an appropriate theme for archaeological research into labor. Extraction of raw materials such as ores and timber transformed the environment and changed the landscape through such additions as tailings piles and slag heaps. Archaeological investigation of the theme "Changing the Role of the United States in the World Community" may address the topics of commerce and immigration/emigration policies. The presence of numerous immigrants employed as a cheap labor source influenced national policies and changed international dynamics as workers left their homelands for opportunities in the United States.

Multiple Property Document

Many states develop contexts for submission to the National Register as multiple property submission (MPS) cover documents. A few examples of such submissions are "Industrial Resources of Huntingdon County MPS" in Pennsylvania, "Yamasee Indian Towns in the South Carolina Low Country MPS," "Great Lakes Shipwrecks MPS" in Wisconsin, and "Chinese Sites in the Warren Mining District MPS" in Idaho. A more complete list of archaeological MPS documents can be found in the *National Register Bulletin* on evaluating archaeological properties (Little et al. 2000). The multiple property format requires discussions of at least one historic context and property types. Acceptance of the multiple property document by the State Historic Preservation Officer (SHPO) and/or Keeper of the National Register means that the property types in the geographic area covered by the multiple property document will be evaluated using the registration requirements defined in the multiple property document. The value of the multiple property approach is that it allows for the coexistence of eligible districts and individually eligible resources within the geographic area defined in the context. Acceptance of the multiple property document by the Keeper of the National Register does not place properties on the NRHP; rather it recognizes the historic context and possibilities of future nominations under the context. The process of evaluating the eligibility of individual nominations, which are prepared with reference to the MPS, concludes with a set of rules or "registration requirements" for determining whether a property is or is not eligible. Eligibility rules are written to apply to each property type.

For example, the MPS "Bright Leaf (Tobacco) Era Farmhouses, North Carolina," specifies that an eligible dwelling should retain a rural setting and the designs, floor plans, or materials that evoke their period of construction, and the rural life of the time should retain a significant degree of stylistic integrity. Integrity of association and feeling is bolstered by the presence of outbuildings, especially those associated with tobacco farming. In an MPS on the Pennsylvania Canal System, canal resources must be associated with an important transportation route or industry in the county to be significant under criterion A. Canal resources must retain integrity of location, design, materials, and association. A portion of the canal right-of-way must retain the visible appearance of an earthen ditch, and locks or dams must be sufficiently intact to represent their original function.

Using State Comprehensive Preservation Plans

State historic preservation offices have gathered information and have developed contexts that may be used to help evaluate archaeological resources. While some contexts may have been formatted as multiple property submissions, as discussed previously, many have not. In many cases the state contexts provide useful examples of research needs for archaeological resources within the state. Such needs may be cited as justification for particular information being described as important when arguing for criterion D for an archaeological site or district. Typically state plans define which historic contexts need to be written for the state. As new areas of history become recognized as important and as new questions are asked of archaeological resources, contexts need to be updated. States vary in how they go about developing and updating contexts. Before attempting to update contexts, one should check with the SHPO or other preservation office for current contexts and research needs. For example, the *Nevada Comprehensive Preservation Plan* (White et al. 1991) defines several study units for developing historic contexts at the state or local level. There are a number of contexts developed and currently used. Each state context is organized around time, theme, and place. The plan's study units, historic contexts, and details on the railroad context are shown in table 2.4.

Context Step 3: Define Property Types

The key link between the historic context of a property and the property itself is the property type. The *National Register Bulletin* on completing the Multiple Property Documentation form (NPS 1991b) defines property type as "a grouping of individual properties characterized by common physical and/or associative attributes." They include the physical remains of buildings used as workers' housing, buildings used as banks, flumes used to transport lumber, plantations, stage stations, and pottery kilns. The *National Register Bulletin* on historic mining properties (Noble and Spude 1992: 9ff), for example, suggests some categories of property types associated with the three fundamental stages in mineral processing—extraction, beneficiation, and refining—as well as

Table 2.4   Nevada State Comprehensive Preservation Plan

Study Units

land usage
  Ranching and farming
  Reclamation and irrigation
  Townsite development and city planning
  Historic landscapes
  The public domain
transportation and communication
government and politics
the people
social organizations and movements
literature, arts, and journalism

Contexts Currently Completed

Railroads of Nevada
Mining and mining-related: the Comstock Era
Ranching and farming in Nevada
Military in Nevada
Education in Nevada
State and county government
Blacks in Nevada
British and Irish
Chinese and Japanese
Utopian communities in Nevada
Newspapers on the Comstock Era

The Railroad Context

Time periods:
  1867–83 First period of major construction
  1883–1902 Period of minimum construction
  1902–14 Second period of major construction
  1914–30 Limited growth with some abandonment
  1930– Short lines abandoned; railroad consolidation and restructuring
Railroad-related themes and subthemes:
  Land usage: townsite development and city planning
  Transportation and communication: exploration and early settlement,
    commercial overland, automobile, maritime
  Commerce and industry: nineteenth century mining, early twentieth century
    mining, tourism
  Government and politics: military
  The people: British and Irish, Chinese, Italians, Japanese, Mexicans

property types associated with engineer-designed complexes, mining landscapes, and related properties such as entire communities. Specific property types depend upon the specific type and development of mining in an area. For example, beneficiation, which is the upgrading of ore, includes many metallurgical processes, which will vary according to the type of ore, technology, and time period. In some cases, the significance of properties may be enhanced by associated properties. For example, prospect holes resulting from the exploration phase of extraction may acquire additional significance to that associated with the mining speculation if there are adjacent camps with archaeological evidence that helps to reconstruct the history of the mining property.

It is often difficult for archaeologists to use historic contexts to evaluate the archaeological significance of historical sites. The most difficult problem is making the connections between archaeological resources and property types. Two linking concepts that can be used to help make the connections are the "feature system" and the "sociotechnical system."

Feature Systems

Donald Hardesty (1988: 9–11) defines the feature system as one linking concept for transforming archaeological resources into property types. Feature systems are networks or geographical clusters of archaeological features that can be linked to the same human activity, such as a technological process or a specific social organization, for example, a household. The feature system is defined by combining archaeology, history, and ethnography and is used as an interpretive tool; in some ways it is similar to the site complex defined by Lewis Binford (1983: 117) for interpreting the archaeology of hunting and gathering sites. Documentary or ethnographic images of a technological process such as pan amalgamation metallurgy, for example, are used as models to identify and interpret archaeological features that are associated with the process. The surviving physical remains, in turn, are used to elaborate and modify the documentary and ethnographic images of the technology. Feature systems are defined by working within this interactive framework. The definition of feature systems often crosscuts

Table 2.5　Possible Property Types Based on Three Stages of Mineral Processing (Abstracted from Noble and Spude 1992: 10–13)

I. Prospecting/Mine Exploration Property Types:
Hand-dug prospect pits
Power-shovel trenches
Bulldozer cuts
Drill holes

II. Mine Development and Exploitation Property Types:
Hoisting works such as headframes and hoist engines
Open pits, shafts, or adits
Ventilation systems such as air shafts or blowers
Power systems such as steam boilers or electric generator houses
Drainage systems such as Cornish pumps
Water delivery systems
Ore bins or tipples
Transportation systems such as short line railroads or ore cart runways
Maintenance and administrative facilities such as blacksmith shops,
assay laboratories, offices, and workers' housing

III. Beneficiation Property Types
Arrastras
Mills
Concentrators
Smelters
Leaching tanks

IV. Refining Property Types
Assay offices
Private banks
Express offices
Mints
Other refineries

archaeological sites if a relatively long time period is represented. Feature systems are the physical remains of synchronic processes or organizations, but the archaeological record is the cumulative end product of all past human activities at the site. Mines, for example, are archaeological sites that might include the physical remains of hoisting works from different time periods and using different technologies. In the 1860s the most typical hoisting system was a whim, followed in the 1870s by steam-driven hoist engine systems in the deep underground mines and in the 1890s by the introduction of an electric-engine driven system. Each of these hoisting systems is defined as a separate feature system.

Sociotechnical Systems

Another example of a linking concept is the sociotechnical system. Historian of technology Thomas Hughes (1983) defined the concept to explain the emergence of modern electrical power. He argues that modern electrical power must be understood within a technological, scientific, economic, political, and social context that defines the system. Thomas Edison, for example, created the system by seeking to supply electrical power at a price competitive with gas (economic), obtain the support of key politicians (political), cut down the cost of transmitting power (engineering), and finding a bulb filament of sufficiently high resistance (scientific). Anthropologist Brian Pfaffenberger (1992) argues that such sociotechnical systems provide the proper context for the study of technology. He defines (1992: 497) the sociotechnical system as "the distinctive technological activity that stems from the linkage of techniques and material culture to the social coordination of labor." Technique, in turn, is defined as a "system of material resources, tools, operational sequences and skills, verbal and nonverbal knowledge, and specific modes of work coordination that come into play in the fabrication of material artifacts" (Pfaffenberger 1992: 497). The beliefs, attitudes, and values making up the work culture also play an important part in the system.

Overland roads, for example, can be usefully conceptualized in a similar way as a technological system that links together techniques (tools, knowledge, operational sequences, and skills), material culture, and the social coordination of labor in a distinctive way. Techniques include road-engineering methods (e.g., construction of the roadbed with hand tools or mechanical grader) and transport technology such as road vehicles (e.g., animal-drawn or steam-powered) and traffic support (e.g., way stations). The social coordination of labor includes such things as kinship and camaraderie networks (e.g., construction/improvement of overland emigration wagon roads), proprietary capitalism (e.g., toll roads constructed and operated by individual entrepreneurs), corporate capitalism (e.g., road corporations), and government transportation policy (e.g., the Lincoln Highway).

Context Step 4: Identify Further Information Needs

In the development of any historic context, there will be further information needs. New questions appear in relevant literature, new issues arise, and new information comes to light. For archaeological contexts, the identification of further information needs is closely tied to research designs and the definition of important information under criterion D.

Many of the general themes in the NPS thematic framework will appear familiar to archaeologists. In practice, most research in historical archaeology, whether grounded in scientific theory or humanistic interpretation, attempts to answer many of the same questions about the human condition in the modern world. For this reason, they tend to have the same problem domains and, therefore, to require the same types of archaeological information, making the task of assessing the information value of historical sites somewhat easier than the plethora of research objectives and explanatory frameworks would suggest. Problem domains are different from historic contexts in that the same problem domain may inspire research questions in different places and times. Historic contexts may touch on several problem domains. The following are some of the common problem domains in historical archaeology.

The Evolution of Technology

The archaeological remains of historical sites often contain data useful in testing theories of technological change. Historian George Basalla (1988), for example, proposed an evolutionary model of technological change that stresses continuity and gradual or cumulative change. In Basalla's model, technological variation and selection within an economic, social, and cultural context are the key processes explaining change. More recently, archaeologist Robert Adams (1996) proposed a competing model based on episodic bursts of rapid technological change associated with social and cultural revolutions.

The Transformation of Everyday Life

Social historians use documents to describe, interpret, and compare everyday life during the past five hundred years. Some anthropologists such as Anthony F. C. Wallace (e.g., in *Rockdale*) do the same. Archaeological data from historical sites potentially provide an enormous repository of information about the transformation of everyday life during the past five hundred years. Historical sites, for example, often contain information about rapid changes taking place in the consumer behavior of U.S. households. Trade and consumer behavior reflect not only world-system changes in the production of material goods but also a distinctive regional pattern of interpretation.

The Archaeology in Annapolis project has researched changes in that Maryland city as the culture of capitalism developed through the eighteenth century. Starting with James Deetz's (1977) observations about the overall cultural change in New England from communal to individual, Mark Leone (e.g., Leone 1988, Leone and Potter 1988) designed the project to focus on capitalism in the search for underlying causes for the culture change. Capitalism evolved as sets of social rules as well as an economic system. Archaeological analysis has identified at least some of the ways in which class relationships are negotiated through material culture within this culture of capitalism. The use of space, including the city plan, landscape, and gardens, is one of the ways in which people negotiate and effect changing cultural norms and social rules. Leone's analysis of William Paca's formal garden in the city hinges on the idea that ideological beliefs are expressed in the built landscape (e.g., Leone 1984). Several researchers in the project have also explored landscape symbolism in the baroque town plan and formal gardens and connected such symbolism to changing social rules (e.g., Leone and Shackel 1990, Kryder-Reid 1991, Shackel et al. 1998).

Barbara Little has examined the intersection of emerging print culture and capitalism through the study of the Green family of printers who worked in Annapolis from the 1730s to the 1830s (e.g.,

Little 1994b, 1998). The material culture expressions of that intersection are seen at several scales of the built environment, from regional economic and political power shifts and correlated locations of printing businesses, to the city plan and the movement of print shops around the city, to the organization of the house lot itself. The separation of home space from workspace is one of the markers of a changing cultural common sense that focuses on the individual rather than on the community. Changing gender ideology and behavior also come into play. Little analyzes the changes in the print shop and house and the differences between probate inventories between the death of Jonas Green in 1767 and the death of his widow and successor, Anne Catherine Green, in 1775. She suggests that, as an expression of a gender-influenced preference for a particular cultural metaphor, Anne Catherine Green followed a domestic task orientation rather than the emergent wage-labor time orientation expressed by her husband (Little 1994b).

Environmental Change in the Modern World

The Industrial Revolution brought with it dramatic changes not only in society and culture but also in the physical environment. Since then, industry-induced environmental changes in the modern world have occurred, and continue to occur, with increasing frequency and intensity (e.g., Adams 1996). In many ways, they are equivalent to the environmental changes brought about by large-scale natural events such as volcanic eruptions. Perhaps the most dramatic example of industry-induced environmental change, however, is the discharge of toxic wastes or other materials that change the chemical composition of air, soil, and water. Historian Duane Smith in his book *Mining America,* for example, writes that the nineteenth-century iron and copper smelting industry in Ducktown, Tennessee, belched out toxic fumes that "killed the vegetation and made the soil barren for miles around" (Smith 1987: 97). The large number, variability, and range of industry-induced environmental changes that have taken place over the past three hundred years suggest that industrial archaeology is well positioned to enhance our knowledge of global change. This, as Carole Crumley (1994: 5), in her introduction to the book *Historical Ecology,* wrote a few years ago, is facilitated by documenting multiple regional environmental changes; in turn, these regional environmental histories can identify sensitive geographical locations for both human and other living populations. Interregional relationships may then be established and integrated with global data.

In addition to being diverse and abundant, industrial sites are high-resolution historical analogs of environmental changes taking place in time periods as short as a few months to as long as three hundred years. Both written records and industrial landscapes record fine-grained local and regional environmental histories of industry-induced environmental change. The short to moderately long time spans of industrial sites provide environmental records capable of connecting studies of the present with long-term paleoenvironmental studies.

Industry-induced environmental changes, and their archaeological records, occur in geographical places ranging in size from small localities to regions covering several square miles. Patrick Kirch's (1992) archaeological study of modern world environmental changes on the Hawaiian Island of Oahu points to a good geographical model of the places where industry-induced environmental change takes place. Such changes often can be viewed as taking place on conceptual islands and studied using the methods of cross-cultural comparison (e.g., Kirch 1997). The archaeological record of the Anahulu Valley, for example, documents two major episodes of environmental change. Seafaring Polynesians in the third century A.D. brought about the first episode by introducing irrigation-based taro farming and the husbandry of pigs and dogs, which transformed the pristine mesic forest into gardens and second-growth forest. Captain James Cook's voyage to the island in 1778 created the second episode. The introduction of European plants and animals deforested the valley and drastically changed hydrologic patterns by the nineteenth century. Each industrial island is, in effect, a case study of the "sensitivity" of geographical places as a habitat for human occupation. The scale and boundaries of the industrial islands ebb and flow with the technology, its social and cultural context, and its history. Some are long lasting with dramatic signatures, others are fleeting and leave barely a trace. The islands' industry-induced environmental changes vary not only in time and space but also in magnitude and intensity. Industrial archaeology is a critical pathway to documenting the environmental histories of the islands.

Class and Ethnic Group Formation

Some of the most important issues in modern labor history, industrial sociology, and the anthropology of complex societies are focused on the evolution of social hierarchies within social formations such as the community. The world-system paradigm discussed more fully in chapter 3, for example, provides a framework within which to explore the evolution of social hierarchies. Samir Amin (1980), for example, argues that wealth accumulates in peripheries and is concentrated in elite groups. Thus, the formation of new hierarchical social structures, such as those that emerged rapidly in California gold rush mining towns like Nevada City and Grass Valley, is implied by the transformation of the American West into a fully developed periphery.

New ethnic groups often emerge as new places are incorporated into expanding world systems. Perhaps the best example is the emergence of the Mestizo as a distinctive ethnic group in Florida and the American Southwest. Thomas Hall (1989: 210) argues that in New Mexico, for example, the expansion of the American state transformed indigenous Hispanic groups into "an enclaved ethnic group with a distinctive culture and a distinct class position within a larger structure." Similarly, Kathy Deagan (1982) argues that in Florida the common practice of intermarriage between Spanish soldiers and Timucua Indians explains the emergence of the Mestizo as an ethnic group. The Florida system contrasts with the mission system, which forcefully resettled Native Americans around Spanish missions in California and elsewhere and made religious conversion, military force, and social or economic pressures the key to cultural exchange between the two groups.

ELIGIBILITY STEP 3: EVALUATE SIGNIFICANCE UNDER NATIONAL REGISTER CRITERIA A–D

Following the standards and guidelines issued by the secretary of the Interior (U.S. Department of the Interior 1983; 36 CFR 60.4, NPS

1991a), cultural resources are significant if they meet the registration requirements for listing on the National Register of Historic Places. The registration requirements include eligibility under at least one of four significance criteria: integrity; significance at either the local, state, or national level; age of at least fifty years; or being of exceptional value if not meeting any of the other requirements (36 CFR 60.4). The *National Register Bulletin* on evaluating and registering archaeological properties (Little et al. 2000) identifies the circumstances under which the archaeological remains of historical sites may be eligible for listing on the National Register of Historic Places.

The archaeological remains must be important under at least one of four significance criteria (A–D) to be eligible for listing on the National Register (36 CFR 60; 36 CFR 63; NPS 1991c). Furthermore, the "Secretary of Interior's Standards and Guidelines" (U.S. Department of the Interior 1983) stipulate that the four criteria are to be applied within historic contexts. Historic contexts should be developed or expanded for this purpose. As described previously, the contexts identify the thematic, geographical, and chronological framework within which the significance evaluation takes place.

Levels of Significance

The archaeological remains of a historical site may be significant at the national, state, or local level. Historic contexts should identify the types of resources significant at each of these levels. For archaeological sites, the level of significance relies primarily on the scope of the applicable research design. That is, sites that might address questions about local history are of local significance. Those properties that might address questions on a state or regional level are usually classified at the state level of significance, and those that might address questions of national importance could be of national significance. Nominators can make recommendations for national significance, but national significance on a National Register form is different from designation as a National Historic Landmark (NHL). While the keeper of the National Register officially lists properties on the National Register of Historic Places, the secretary of Interior designates nationally significant properties as National Historic Landmarks. The Historic Sites Act of 1935 authorized the Secretary of Interior to recognize as National Historic Landmarks nationally significant properties in United States history and archaeology. The National Historic Preservation Act of 1966 expanded the recognition to properties of state and local significance with the creation of the National Register of Historic Places. Since the establishment of the National Register, all NHLs have been automatically listed. Table 2.6 shows six criteria for NHLs, found in 36 CFR 65. The one most relevant for archeological properties is cri-

Table 2.6   National Historic Landmarks Criteria

The quality of national significance is ascribed to districts, sites, buildings, structures, and objects that possess exceptional value or quality in illustrating or interpreting the heritage of the United States in history, architecture, archeology, engineering, and culture and that possess a high degree of integrity of location, design, setting, materials, workmanship, feeling, and association, and:

1. That are associated with events that have made a significant contribution to, and are identified with, or that outstandingly represent, the broad national patterns of United States history and from which an understanding and appreciation of those patterns may be gained; or
2. That are associated importantly with the lives of persons nationally significant in the history of the United States; or
3. That represent some great idea or ideal of the American people; or
4. That embody the distinguishing characteristics of an architectural type specimen exceptionally valuable for a study of a period, style, or method of construction, or that represent a significant, distinctive, and exceptional entity whose components may lack individual distinction; or
5. That are composed of integral parts of the environment not sufficiently significant by reason of historical association or artistic merit to warrant individual recognition, but collectively compose an entity of exceptional historical or artistic significance or outstandingly commemorate or illustrate a way of life or culture; or
6. That have yielded or may be likely to yield information of major scientific importance by revealing new cultures, or by shedding light on periods of occupation over large areas of the United States. Such sites are those that have yielded, or that may reasonably be expected to yield, data affecting theories, concepts, and ideas to a major degree.

terion 6. See the *National Register Bulletin*, "How to Prepare National Historical Landmark Nominations" for more information.

Applying Significance Criteria

The National Register process applies four criteria in determining whether the archaeological remains of a historical site are significant. Under criteria A, B, and C an archaeological property must have demonstrated its ability to convey its significance. Under criterion D, only the potential to yield important information is required.

Criterion A

The archaeological remains of historical sites are significant under criterion A if they are strongly associated with events that have made a significant contribution to the broad patterns of national, state, or local history. Under criterion A, the site may be significant if the archaeological remains are needed to convey or illustrate or help interpret a historic property strongly associated with an important historical event or pattern. The property's specific association must be considered important. Criterion A evaluation involves the following steps:

Step 1. Identify the associated historical event or pattern.

Step 2. Document the importance of the event or pattern in national, state, or local history.

Step 3. Demonstrate the strength of the association between the event or pattern and the archaeological remains of the historical site.

Step 4. Assess the integrity of the archaeological remains. Do they retain enough integrity of location, setting, and association to convey or illustrate or interpret the property?

Often, archaeological properties that are nominated under criteria A, B, or C in addition to D convey their significance through visible remains. Earthworks dating to the Civil War, for example, are often listed under criterion A. The Blue Springs Encampment and Fortifications in Bradley County, Tennessee, which are associated with General William T. Sherman's army between October 1863 and April 1865, are listed under both criteria A and D. The Old Town Fernandina Historic Site in Nassau County, Florida, is listed under criteria A, C, and D. The nomination documents that it is the last town founded by Spain in North America and it retains the Spanish town plan from its period of significance of 1811–21.

Another example of a historical archaeological property listed under both criteria A and D is the Johnson Ranch and Burtis Hotel Site in Yuba County, California. The archaeological remains of those two buildings and a remnant of the California Trail have a period of significance from 1846 to 1862, when the Johnson Ranch served as both the physical and emotional end of the California Trail. The nomination (Horn 1991) refers to the sense of history imparted by this site because of its association with the Donner Party and several early explorers.

Criterion B

The archaeological remains of a historical site might be significant under criterion B if they are strongly associated with the lives of persons who have made a significant contribution to national, state, or local history. The application of criterion B to archaeological properties usually requires that there are no other properties that represent the person in question. Under criterion B, the archaeological remains might be significant if they are needed to convey or illustrate or interpret a historic property that is strongly associated with the career of an important person. Criterion B evaluation involves the following steps:

Step 1. Identify the important person(s) associated with the property.

Step 2. Document the importance of the person in the context of national, state, or local history.

Step 3. Demonstrate the strength of the association between the person(s) and the property. Did the person live or work on the property during the career for which he or she is recognized?

Step 4. Assess the integrity of the property. Does the property retain enough integrity of location, setting, and association to convey its significance? Would the important person recognize the property today?

An example of an archaeological site listed under criterion B is the Rosemont Plantation in Laurens County, South Carolina (Trinkley 1992). The property is associated with Anne Pamela Cunningham, founder of the Mount Vernon Ladies Association. There is no other property associated with Cunningham. The site has intact grounds and its remaining landscape features, such as brick walls, paths, plantings of boxwood, and specimen trees, retain sufficient integrity as the grounds of her home over her life. The horticultural evidence and the design elements of the landscape are sufficient to convey association with her life despite the fact that the buildings are gone and the grounds are overgrown. Especially important are trees from Mount Vernon planted by her parents, because these served as inspiration from her home and family that influenced her to preserve Mount Vernon.

Criterion C

The archaeological remains of a historical site are significant under criterion C if they embody the distinctive characteristics of a type, period, or method of construction, or represent the work of a master, or possess high artistic values, or represent a significant and distinguishable entity whose components may lack individual distinction. Under criterion C, the archaeological remains may be significant if they are needed to convey to the present or illustrate or interpret a historic property that is strongly associated with a distinctive architectural or engineering pattern or style or type. Criterion C evaluation involves the following steps:

Step 1. Identify the distinctive architectural or engineering characteristics of the property.

Step 2. Document the importance of the architectural or

engineering pattern or type or style in the context of national, state, or local history.

Step 3. Evaluate how strongly the property illustrates the distinctive architectural or engineering characteristics.

Step 4. Assess the integrity of the property. Does it retain enough integrity of design, material, and workmanship to convey or illustrate or interpret the architectural or engineering pattern or type?

As mentioned under criterion A, visible remains of properties more easily convey their significance under criteria other than D. Civil War earthworks and shipwrecks sometimes qualify for listing under criterion C. The Cremaillere Line Fortification in Lake County, Tennessee, is a Confederate earthwork built in August 1862. The remaining 433 yards of this indented earthwork are listed under criteria A, C, and D. The San Felipe Shipwreck Site in Monroe County, Florida, also is listed under criteria A, C, and D. The wreck is representative of a specific type of eighteenth-century merchant vessel architecture and is listed under criterion C for that reason.

When listed in 1992, the Rosemont Plantation did not qualify for listing under criterion C. According to staff comments accompanying the nomination, its significance for landscape architecture was based on the potential of the site to provide information about the nature and design of early nineteenth-century plantations in upland South Carolina. However, the context for this type of resource was not developed such that the property was shown to be a good example of a landscape style or type. Instead the wealth of records and landscape supports criterion D rather than C because they are likely to yield important information.

The South Dakota State Historic Preservation Center (1985) uses the following questions in determining whether mining technology properties are significant under criterion C:

- Is the technological pattern represented by the property the first of its kind?
- Does the property represent a major change in technology?
- Is the technological pattern represented by the property the last of an era?

- Does the property represent a new or experimental approach to technology?
- Is the property a reasonably well-preserved example of a technology that is typical of a period of significance?

Criterion D

The archaeological remains of a historical site are significant if they have yielded, or may be likely to yield, information important in prehistory or history. Under criterion D, archaeological properties might be significant if they are important to scientific or scholarly research. An archaeological site that has been completely excavated no longer contains archaeological information and, therefore, has lost significance under criterion D. The site, however, may still be significant under criterion A if it is strongly associated with, for example, an important scientific or scholarly discovery (e.g., a discovery that revolutionizes ideas about human antiquity in the Americas) or the history of archaeology.

It is important to realize that a property that is listed will not necessarily be investigated according to the research design offered in the National Register nomination. There is no obligation to investigate a property after listing. Because someone has gone to the trouble to recognize significance and then document and nominate a property, there is often more attention paid to its preservation. Therefore, eligible sites may not in fact yield the information they have been judged capable of yielding until some unspecified time in the future. It is quite likely that new research questions and new techniques and methods will have been developed by the time some listed sites are excavated. Criterion D evaluation involves the following steps:

Step 1. Identify the property's data sets or categories of information.

Step 2. Identify appropriate historical and archaeological contexts.

Step 3. Document why the information is important to scientific or scholarly research.

Step 4. Assess the integrity of the property.

Step 5. Identify important information that the property has
    yielded or is likely to yield.

Under steps 1 and 2, the information that the property contains is
identified. Field assessments of the artifacts, ecofacts, features, and
archaeological contexts contained in the archaeological record of
the property are critical. The assessment is best done by combining
on-site surface observations, probing buried deposits, documentary
research, and, where available, oral testimony from persons familiar with the history of the site.

The development of research designs or formal structures of inquiry are critical to step 3. Research designs stipulate the explanatory framework within which questioning takes place, the research
questions that are important within that framework, and the data
requirements of the important research questions. Chapter 3 discusses the procedure in more detail. Next, the strength of the association between the information and the property must be demonstrated. Is the property, for example, the only or most abundant
archaeological repository of the important information?

Under step 4, determine whether the property retains enough integrity of location, design, and association to meet the data requirements of important scientific or scholarly research questions. The
distinction between primary and secondary archaeological deposits
is critical. Secondary deposits, for example, have been moved by
natural or cultural processes from their original place of deposition
and could, therefore, have lost integrity of location under criterion
D. The scale at which questioning, however, takes place is important in assessing integrity in this case (see what follows). A secondary deposit of household trash found at a town dump, for example,
probably has lost integrity of location for answering research questions about households but has retained integrity of location for answering research questions about the town.

There are many examples of sites listed under criterion D, because it is the most common criterion under which archaeological
properties are evaluated and listed. The San Felipe Shipwreck Site
mentioned previously is likely to yield information about specific
methods of its construction. Because of its intact condition, it is also

likely to yield information on social stratification among this ship's passengers, officers, and crew (it wrecked in 1733).

In another example, the Riverside Cemetery in Adams County, Colorado, with its period of significance from 1876 to 1944 contains information on common people in early Denver that is not otherwise available, because there are no systematic records of death until 1910 (Hegner 1994). Archaeology and physical anthropology could provide information about the unidentified dead by addressing such questions as:

- Who were these many people from the early decades of Denver's history?
- What kind of people were neglected or forgotten so soon?
- Did these people belong to particular racial groups?
- What was the state of their health?
- Do the skeletons reveal trauma, or are they free of premortem injury?
- Are the sexes represented disproportionately?
- Is the demographic age distribution at time of death normal or skewed?

Some Unusual Applications of Criterion D Properties that are significant for the important information they may supply to industrial archaeology are often aboveground resources. The Cos Cob Power Station in Fairfield County, Connecticut, is listed under criteria A, C, and D for transportation and industry. Archaeology is not listed as an area of significance, although study of the aboveground resources is likely to yield industrial and engineering data that could shed light on the construction, day-to-day operation, and demise of the station. The Connecticut Valley Railroad in Middlesex, Connecticut, is listed under criteria A and D for transportation and engineering. The remains of the roundhouse and turntable were uncovered archaeologically and are important for the information they are likely to yield about poorly documented railroad maintenance facilities. The Brooklyn Tobacco Factory in Virginia, the best-preserved antebellum property of its kind, is listed under A and D for industry. The equipment, graffiti, chemical residue, and other features of the factory itself provide the source of likely information about factory practice to justify criterion D.

Buildings can be listed under criterion D for the important information they are likely to contain on the construction of the buildings. For example, the MPS "First Period Buildings of Eastern Massachusetts" argues for the eligibility of early buildings under criterion D for their important information about building techniques. In the multiple property submission "Iron and Steel Resources in Pennsylvania, 1716–1945," properties might be listed under criterion D not only for the likely information to be discovered belowground but also for the information contained in the size and configuration of the buildings.

There are some other types of properties that are listed under criterion D that do not list archaeology as an area of significance. There are, for example, two World War II Launch sites in Okaloosa County, Florida, listed for their military significance. The wreckage of missiles tested there could provide information on this highly classified project, which was essential to the development of modern cruise missiles. In another case, the Shockoe Hill Cemetery in Richmond, Virginia, is listed under criteria C and D for art and social history but not for archaeology of the belowground resources. The studies of ornamentation, symbolism, and inscriptions are expected to yield information on social history, such as social standing, attitudes toward death and spiritual beliefs, prevalence of fraternal organizations, and the craft of artisans in iron and stone.

Are Historic Trash Dumps Significant?   Among the more controversial issues in making significance determinations is whether or not a domestic or industrial trash dump is significant. In most instances, it is unlikely that a trash dump is significant by itself; however, they often contribute to the significance of associated properties or as one of a larger group of trash dumps. Once again, the scale of the significance evaluation is critical. Secondary trash dumps associated with a townsite, for example, may be significant under criterion D as a repository of archaeological information about changing patterns of consumer behavior in the town during its period of significance. The trash dumps, however, are not significant repositories of information about the households where the consumption actually took place because the trash has been transported and redeposited elsewhere and therefore cannot be associated with individual households.

Domestic and industrial trash dumps typically acquire significance under criterion D as repositories of archaeological information important to scientific and scholarly research. Certainly, for example, they might shed light on questions about variability and change in the consumer behavior of social groups or the details of technological processes. But trash dumps also may be significant under the other criteria because they help convey or illustrate or interpret the historical importance of associated properties. Under criterion A, for example, visible domestic trash dumps associated with an African-American farmstead may help illustrate or interpret the importance of the property in national, state, or local history by adding critical information about the lifeways of the people who once lived on the property and conveying information about the inhabitants' life during the period of significance.

Under criterion B, trash dumps could help convey the importance of persons in national, state, and local history by fleshing out their careers or work or lifeways. Simeon Wenban, for example, one of Hubert H. Bancroft's Kings of Industry (Bancroft 1889), lived his productive life in the Cortez mining district of central Nevada from the 1860s to the 1890s. Domestic trash dumps associated with his house in the 1880s provide important clues to his lifestyle as a Victorian gentleman on the mining frontier and document his unique social and cultural position in this remote frontier mining community. If not significant in their own right, Wenban's trash dumps certainly contribute to the significance of his house as a property.

Trash dumps, finally, sometimes contribute to the criterion C significance of a property by conveying the importance of an architectural or an engineering pattern or style or type. Industrial refuse from a pottery kiln, for example, may provide enough new information about the technology used to make a strong case for the kiln's significance as a unique pottery manufacturing process and also visibly convey the organization of workspace.

Traditional Cultural Properties   A traditional cultural property (TCP) is a property that is associated with cultural practices or beliefs of a living community that 1) are rooted in that community's history and 2) are important in maintaining the continuing cultural identity of the community. (Parker and King 1998: 1). TCPs are not usually archaeological, but archaeologists are likely to come across these places. TCPs are not special kinds of properties, and they are not new. Places of traditional importance that meet at least one of the eligibility criteria have been listed in the National Register nearly from the beginning of the program.

It is not always easy to distinguish between traditional cultural places that are eligible for listing in the National Register and those that are not. A TCP must be important to the community today and must have served for at least fifty years in the same role. The period of significance must come up to the present. Indeed, the period of significance is one of the main differences between TCPs and other eligible properties. The use of the property does not have to be continuous but the association must be direct.

The property must be a tangible place and not simply a practice. This does not mean that cultural modifications need to have occurred. The association between the property and the community must be strong. If a practice can be carried out somewhere else, then there is not a sufficient link between the place and the practice to justify eligibility. Defensible boundaries should be based on the property's characteristics, how it is used, and why it is important.

The El Cerro Tome site in Valencia County, New Mexico, is a religious ceremonial site with an estimated period of significance from 3000 B.C. to A.D. 1945. The hill has played a spiritual role in the lives of local Pueblo and Hispanic peoples. At the summit of a volcanic plug rising about four hundred feet above the surrounding land are a shrine and four crosses (calvario), the destination of current religious pilgrimages. Along the trails are numerous prehistoric and historic petroglyphs and possible shrines as well as room blocks and masonry structures. Its greatest visitation is on Good Friday when people from the local area begin a procession to the summit. Several thousand pilgrims reach the calvario, offer their prayers, and depart. Oral tradition maintains that pueblos from Isleta conducted ceremonies there as late as the early 1900s. In the mid-nineteenth century the Penitente Brotherhood began holding Good Friday services on El Cerro Tome. The tradition died out by the mid-twentieth century but has been recently revived. ''Residents maintain that they derive a strong sense of place from the nearby hill, and that they turn to the hill for spiritual strength and healing" (Kammer 1995: 8).

El Tiradito (Wishing Shrine) is in one of Tucson's oldest Mexican-American neighborhoods. In spite of the religious significance, the shrine embodies a cultural legacy, which is part of the Mexican-American heritage. This site does not have the official sanction of the Catholic Church. The shrine pertains to the belief that certain of the dead may grant wishes to living persons who light votive candles for them. The dead person to whom the shrine was erected was a social outcast within the community. El tiradito means "the outcast or castaway" (Garrison 1975).

An eligible property that is not listed in the National Register is the Virgin Island in Assumption Parish, Louisiana. It is a small island that has been the site of traditional devotions to the Virgin Mary practiced by the residents of the eastern Atchafalaya Basin area in Louisiana since 1872. The shrine itself is not considered eligible since the statue and its setting have been altered several times. The island is an important symbol of the community as an essential component of ethnic and community identity. The island as her shrine exemplifies the strong devotion of this Acadian community to the Virgin Mary. The island is viewed as a particularly appropriate place to ask for intercession and to give thanks. It is the site of an annual mass and boat blessing conducted by the Church of St. Joseph the Worker.

ELIGIBILITY STEP 4: APPLY CRITERIA CONSIDERATIONS

The National Register normally excludes certain property types from eligibility. They include birthplaces, cemeteries and graves, religious properties, properties moved from their original location, reconstructed buildings and structures, commemorative properties, and properties less than fifty years old. Archaeological resources associated with these property types are treated in the same way. Under some circumstances, however, they are eligible for listing on the National Register. They are eligible, for example, if they are a key element of a historic district or if they meet one of the following conditions (NPS 1991c: 2):

a. a religious property deriving primary significance from architectural or artistic distinction or historical importance;
b. a building or structure removed from its original location but which is significant primarily for architectural value, or which is the surviving structure most importantly associated with a historic person or event;
c. a birthplace or grave of a historical figure of outstanding importance, if there is no appropriate site or building directly associated with his or her productive life;
d. a cemetery that derives its primary significance from graves of persons of transcendent importance, from age, from distinctive design features, from associations with historic events;
e. a reconstructed building when accurately executed in a suitable environment and presented in a dignified manner as part of a restoration master plan, and when no other building or structure with the same association has survived;
f. a property primarily commemorative in intent if design, age, tradition, or symbolic value has invested it with its own exceptional significance; or
g. a property achieving significance within the past fifty years if it is of exceptional significance.

It is not necessary to apply the criteria considerations if a property is an integral part of a district or site that meets the criteria. For example, if a family cemetery is included in a district that contains a historic farmstead, then it is not necessary to address criteria consideration d. Similarly, a cemetery that is nominated under criterion D for information value does not need to meet the criteria consideration.

ELIGIBILITY STEP 5: DETERMINE IF PROPERTY RETAINS SUFFICIENT INTEGRITY TO CONVEY ITS SIGNIFICANCE

In addition to eligibility under at least one of the four significance criteria, the archaeological remains also must have retained enough integrity to convey their significance to people in the present. The National Register identifies seven elements of integrity: location, design, setting, materials, workmanship, feeling, and association (NPS 1991c).

All properties must be able to convey their significance. Under criterion D, properties convey this by the information they contain. The National Register emphasizes that under criteria A, B, and C a property must look much like it did during its period of significance. Integrity of setting and feeling usually increase the "recognizability" of a property. Under criteria A and B, the presence or absence of the historic fabric of standing buildings and structures is most important. The elements of location, design, materials, and association are considered to be most important, but the integrity of workmanship, setting, and feeling also are considered. If the building or structure is considered to be significant under criterion C, the integrity elements of workmanship, materials, and design are considered to be most important. Location, for example, is not considered to be an important element of integrity for mining properties, since buildings often were moved and in many cases were intentionally designed to be moved.

Archaeologists use integrity to describe the quality of information contained within an archaeological property. For properties eligible under criterion D, integrity relates directly to the types of research questions defined within the research design. Generally, integrity cannot be thought of as an absolute quality of a property. Instead, it is relative to the specific significance, which is the important information that the property conveys.

To assess integrity, one should do the following.

Step 1. Determine the essential physical qualities that must be present if the property is to represent its significance.

Step 2. Determine if those qualities are discernible enough to convey their significance.

Step 3. With reference to the relevant historic context(s), determine if the property needs to be compared with similar properties, which might be necessary with particularly rare properties.

Step 4. Based on the significance and physical qualities,

determine what aspects of integrity are vital to the property and whether they are present.

Visibility and Focus

In his classic book *In Small Things Forgotten* (1977), James Deetz introduced the concepts of visibility and focus as measures of the integrity of archaeological sites. Visibility refers to the relative abundance of material remains. It is the extent to which the physical remains of a historic property have survived and are observable today. Focus is the degree to which the physical remains are readable or interpretable and can be linked to the historic property (v. Deetz 1977: 94–5). For example, does a property contain the mixed deposits of several occupations and time periods, or the intact remains of a single occupation during a short time period? These concepts of visibility and focus may be used to assess the extent to which historical archaeological sites have retained integrity. Under criteria A–C, all of which require that archaeological remains be capable of conveying or illustrating historic properties, both good visibility and focus are needed. However, to be considered eligible or contributing under criterion D requires only good focus and does not require visibility. The property must be a significant and focused or interpretable repository of information needed to answer one or more of the questions defined in the research design. In many but not all cases, the property must contain a substantial buried or surface archaeological deposit that is relatively undisturbed. The property also must be associated with the place and time period of the historic context.

Scale of Comparison

Particularly for archaeological sites, integrity is a relative concept. James Deetz, in the introduction to *Historical Archaeology in Global Perspective* (1991), observes that the use of the comparative method in historical archaeology requires careful attention to the scale to be used in making comparisons with archaeological data. Mining sites, for example, often are highly disturbed and no longer contain the detailed information about the specific provenience/location of archaeological remains needed to answer specific research questions, such as those involved with local or family history. Yet when asking research questions on a much broader regional, national, or international scale, the archaeological information from these same disturbed sites gains a new significance. Thus, artifact assemblages from heavily disturbed sites of short-duration mining towns in the American West that have been moved from their original sites might not tell us much about specific families or individuals living in the towns but can be an important source of information about other questions.

National Register Elements of Integrity

The National Register defines seven elements of integrity with a clearly architectural bias (NPS 1991c: 44–5). Still, the elements may be used in assessing archaeological integrity. Table 2.7 shows the seven elements of integrity.

To have integrity of location, the property must retain its historic place of significance. Integrity of location is linked closely with integrity of association. In some cases that place of significance may not be a fixed location. For example, integrity of location would not necessarily preclude the eligibility of redeposited materials.

Table 2.7   National Register Elements of Integrity

Location: "the place where the historic property was constructed or the place where the historic event occurred" (NPS 1991c: 44).

Design: "the combination of elements that create the form, plan, space, structure, and style of a property" (NPS 1991c: 44).

Setting: "physical environment of an historic property" (NPS 1991c: 45).

Materials: "the physical elements that were combined or deposited during a particular period of time and in a particular pattern or configuration to form a historic property" (NPS 1991c: 45).

Workmanship: "the physical evidence of the crafts of a particular culture or people during any given period in history or prehistory" (NPS 1991c: 45).

Feeling: "a property's expression of the aesthetic or historic sense of a particular period of time" (NPS 1991c: 45).

Association: "the direct link between an important historic event or person and a historic property" (NPS 1991c :45).

Portable buildings in mining districts may not require integrity of location if they retain integrity of setting.

Criterion C in particular requires integrity of design. To have integrity of design, the property must retain the material expression of plan, layout, style, or cognitive image. Under criterion D, the integrity of design applies to intrasite patterning, or in the case of districts, intersite patterning. Design may be illustrated by the plan or layout of a company town, plantation, engineered mine complex, ethnic landscape, railroad, or some other transportation network.

To have integrity of setting under criteria A and B, the property must retain the physical environment that it had during its time of significance and place of significance. Landscape and viewsheds are important. In the American West, open pit mining often creates the greatest challenge to determining whether or not integrity of setting has been or will be retained. A lack of integrity of setting does not usually impact the potential for important information, but it usually does affect eligibility under criteria A, B, or C.

To have integrity of materials, which is especially important under criterion C, the property must have retained the combination, pattern, or configuration of materials. Under criterion D, integrity of materials is usually described as the completeness or quality of the artifact assemblage and feature preservation.

Criterion C in particular requires integrity of workmanship. To have integrity, the property must have retained evidence of how the craft was produced. Milling and manufacturing are good examples. Under criterion D a pottery kiln would have integrity of workmanship if there were enough of the kiln remaining to illustrate how the pottery was fired. The importance of workmanship depends upon the archaeological resource and the research questions associated with it.

A property has integrity of feeling if "its features in combination with its setting convey a historic sense of the property during its period of significance" (NPS 1991c: 45).

A property retains integrity of association if it is actually the place where the event or activity occurred and it is intact enough to clearly convey the relationship to an observer. Criteria A and B require integrity of association. Under criterion D, integrity of association is judged by the strength of the relationship between the site's content and the important research questions.

NOMINATING PROPERTIES TO THE NATIONAL REGISTER

The first step in nominating properties is identifying them. Potentially eligible properties often are identified through survey projects sponsored by federal, state, or local governments. Such projects often include evaluation of potentially eligible properties. Anyone—professional organizations, historical societies, private property owners, nonprofit organizations, agencies, or individuals—can identify a potentially eligible property and work with the appropriate nominating authority to recognize it through National Register listing.

Properties are nominated by State Historic Preservation Officers (SHPO), Tribal Historic Preservation Officers (THPO), or Federal Preservation Officers (FPO), depending on the location of the property. Nominations are submitted to a state review board, made up of professionals in history, architectural history, archaeology, and other relevant disciplines. The board makes a recommendation to the SHPO to approve or disapprove the nomination. While the property is being reviewed, property owners and local government officials are notified and given the opportunity to comment. Private property owners whose property is included in the nomination have the opportunity to object to the nomination. If a majority of private property owners object to listing, then there can be no formal listing of the property. Any objection by public owners is not relevant to the ability to list a property. Instead, the SHPO would forward the nomination to the keeper of the National Register with a request for a determination of eligibility (DOE). If a majority of private property owners do not object and the preservation officer recommends eligibility, then the nomination is forwarded to the Keeper of the National Register at the National Park Service to be considered for listing.

Preparing a Nomination

When preparing a nomination it is important to consult the guidance that is available in the *National Register Bulletins*. The bulletins

as well as blank forms are available on the Internet at http://www.
cr.nps.gov/nr/publications/bulletins.htm. The bulletin *Guidelines
for Evaluating and Registering Archeological Properties* (Little et al.
2000) along with the basic bulletins on applying the criteria and
completing registration forms are designed to guide the preparation of useful and complete nominations. For assistance on documenting boundaries, see especially the appendix, "Definition of
National Register Boundaries for Archeological Properties," in the
bulletin *How to Define Boundaries for National Register Properties*
(Seifert 1997).

Sample nominations are also available. The National Register has
a collection of good examples that are available. See "Other Guidance" on the website just noted. The SHPO or other preservation
officer can provide samples of accepted nominations as well. The
National Register Information System (NRIS) is available over the
Internet (www.cr.nps.gov/nr/nrcollec.html). The NRIS database
can be downloaded and searched with any search engine by basic
data categories such as site function, period of significance, area of
significance, and cultural affiliation. Certain information, such as
specific locational information for most archaeological properties is
not included. Such information is restricted because of the harm its
release could cause to the resource from trophy hunters, vandals,
and unauthorized searches. Section 304 of the NHPA allows for the
restriction of certain types of information if release of the information would (1) cause a significant invasion of privacy, (2) risk
harm to the historic resource, or (3) impede the use of a traditional
religious site by practitioners.

When preparing nominations, one should also be sure to consult
with the appropriate historic preservation office, whether state, federal, or tribal. The technical requirements are designed to ensure an
"archivally stable" National Register. Therefore one should be sure
to follow such instructions as proper labeling on photographs and
USGS maps. Boundaries should be clearly indicated on maps, because potential effects on properties require defensible boundaries.
Complete forms with appropriate maps will make it much easier
for the archaeologist to successfully work with National Register
staff in historic preservation offices, because such individuals often
have different training and expertise.

We are convinced from years of reviewing nominations that archaeologists tend to be better at describing properties than at justifying their significance. When completing the narrative sections of the form, it would be helpful to think about the audiences for the documentation: decision makers and the general public as well as other archaeologists. In plain language, one should tell the reader what would be lost if the property were to be destroyed and why the loss would matter.

In some cases the historic preservation office requests preliminary reviews of nominations so that potential problems can be identified before formal submission. Such review is often helpful, but it is not subject to the same time deadlines as pertain to formally submitted nominations.

Review at the National Register

Technical Review

To ensure that the technical and administrative information is complete and accurate, all nominations undergo an initial technical review. This review ensures, for example, that the nomination is signed by an authorized official, that information in the text matches that on the cover form, and that adequate photographs and maps have been provided. After technical review, the nomination may be returned to the nominator for correction, listed in the National Register, or forwarded to a staff member for substantive review.

Substantive Review

National Register staff reviewers who are historians and architectural historians are assigned to work with particular states and U.S. territories. The staff archaeologist works with all archaeological nominations. These staff reviewers provide substantive review for nominations in a number of cases. For example, documentation of properties for which a majority of owners object to nomination are forwarded to the staff reviewer(s) for DOE. If determined eligible, a property receives the same protection under the NHPA as if it were formally listed on the National Register. All appeals filed under 36 CFR 60.12 receive substantive review. Nominating authorities may request substantive review. In addition, technical review may reveal the need for substantive review. The nominating authority may also request substantive review of particular properties. For example, a SHPO may request substantive review of a newly recognized category of property with which the staff have little experience and thereby receive additional guidance from the National Park Service.

Acting on Nominations

The National Register must act within forty-five days of receipt. Upon receipt of a nomination, a staff member stamps it with the date of receipt. Notice is placed in the *Federal Register* for a fifteen-day public comment period. Review takes place after this comment period. By the forty-fifth day, a nomination is listed in the National Register if it meets the criteria for evaluation and the documentation requirements. Notice of listing is provided to the nominating authority.

If the property does not meet the criteria, it is rejected. If the nomination does not adequately document the property or explain its significance under the criteria, then it is returned to the nominator. If the documentation is sufficient to evaluate the property but contains minor technical problems, the staff reviewer can correct the nomination and list it by preparing a supplementary listing record (SLR) that is added to the official record.

The SLR is prepared as a National Register continuation sheet. It is used when questions about documentation can be clarified with a telephone (or E-mail) consultation with the nominator. SLRs correct such matters as incorrect UTM (Universal Transverse Mercator) coordinates, missing recommendation for level of significance, counting errors of contributing and noncontributing resources, or missing cultural affiliation for nominations submitted under criterion D.

3

Scientific and Scholarly Significance

Of the four significance criteria used in National Register evaluation, criterion D is most often used to justify the archaeological significance of historical sites. Criterion D stipulates that a property is significant if it "has yielded, or may be likely to yield, information important in prehistory or history." Evaluating historical sites under criterion D requires, first, identifying the information content of the archaeological record and, second, determining the importance of that information to scientific and scholarly research. The evaluation should make the best connection possible between the research questions important to science or to scholarship in general and the information potential of the archaeological record.

WHAT IS ARCHAEOLOGICAL INFORMATION?

In the most general sense, archaeological information exists at three interpretive levels (Hardesty 1995: 4–5). One level consists of field observations of artifacts, features, and other physical remains in archaeological context. Contextual information of this type includes descriptions of provenience, associations, and physical matrix. It also includes descriptions of site size and layout, relative abundance and diversity of physical remains, and data sets based on similarities in material, shape, or other dimensions of form. The second level is where most archaeological questions are addressed and comes into play with the data requirements of research questions derived from middle range explanations that link archaeologi-

53

cal context to past human activities (e.g., Binford 1983, Leone 1988, Schiffer 1987). Examples include the information needed to answer questions about site formation processes, foodways, ancient environments, population size, domestic architecture, and household form and activities. The questions addressed at this level may not be those of anthropological synthesis, but they are the essential building blocks for most of our general research objectives (to be discussed later). At this level, archaeological information exists only after the formulation of research questions that need specific information to answer. The same is true of the third level of archaeological information, which comes from the data requirements of research questions derived from general theories or interpretations, such as cultural evolution, historical materialism, and symbolism. Each of these levels affects the others. For example, both the small and large questions we attempt to answer through archaeological research influence what we look for and what we literally find in the ground. Similarly, observation of unexpected artifacts and features influences the questions we ask. Assessing the archaeological value of historical sites must take into account all three levels of information.

WHAT ARE THE SOURCES OF ARCHAEOLOGICAL INFORMATION?

Archaeological information is contained within the physical remains of past human activities and their archaeological context. The sources of information include artifacts, ecofacts, features, and contexts.

Historical Artifacts

In their textbook *Historical Archaeology,* Charles Orser and Brian Fagan (1995: 75–93) classify the information content of artifacts from historical sites into the categories of historical documents, commodities, and ideas. As historical documents, artifacts provide information about technology, time period, use, and other things. Perhaps the most obvious are artifacts marked with the name or symbol of their manufacturer. Thus ceramic vessels, glass bottles, and tin cans often carry makers' marks in the period after the Industrial Revolution. English pottery between 1842 and 1883, for example, often carry diamond-shaped registry marks with a date, showing that the manufacturer had registered the vessel design or shape with the Patent Office in London at that time. Some artifacts also carry U.S. patent numbers. Also, many artifacts from historical sites show the technology used in their manufacture. The rapid technological change that took place during and after the Industrial Revolution often makes it possible to use technological attributes to date artifacts. Glass bottle technology, for example, changes from free blown to hand blown into molds to machine blown. Pontil marks, seams, and finish attributes reflect the changes.

The second kind of information from artifacts that must be considered is their use as commodities with exchange value. Both documents and historical sites contain information about artifacts as commodities. Documentary sources include probate records, advertisements, trade and retail catalogs, and store inventories.

Many archaeologists use artifacts as commodities to study consumer behavior of different social classes. Traditional expectations that high status translates into large quantities or more expensive household goods, however, are not always met. In their study of the Aiken Plateau in South Carolina, Melanie Cabak and Mary Inkrot found that wealthier households might spend more on services such as domestic help and gasoline but that most households in a community would spend similar amounts on consumer goods. "Although very few households could afford to mechanize their farmsteads or modernize their homes, most people, regardless of tenure class, had access to inexpensive consumer goods, such as soda pop, that were being produced by the nation's expanding factories" (Cabak and Inkrot 1997: 190). Historical archaeologists often use a straightforward but misleading correlation between status and the cost of goods. Charles LeeDecker (1994: 348) writes, "A weakness of many archaeological studies of consumer behavior is the preoccupation with socioeconomic status and inattention to characteristics of the individual households and other factors that influence consumer behavior." Such factors include household composition, life cycle, and income strategy (see Henry 1986).

Finally, the meaning of artifacts to the people who made and used them is the third kind of information they provide. Most of us are familiar with how meaning is used to interpret a few artifacts found at archaeological sites. The excavation of one of the Donner Party's winter campsites in the Sierra Nevada Mountains, for example, found a Roman Catholic religious medal, an obvious symbol of a distinctive set of beliefs that likely carried immense meaning for its user (Hardesty 1997).

Historical Ecofacts

Historical sites also contain information about environments in the form of ecofacts, such as pollen, phytoliths, plant macrofossils, animal bones, and sediments. For example, Paul Shackel (1996) describes three types of archaeobotanical analyses that were carried out to investigate domestic and factory landscapes in Harpers Ferry, West Virginia. Macrofloral studies of fruits and vegetable seeds, pollen analysis of a wider range of plants, and phytoliths mainly from grasses have helped reconstruct historical vegetation patterns. Gardens and manicured lawns characterized the armory grounds in the early nineteenth century. By the 1840s, however, the landscape had deteriorated as the industrial character of the town took precedence over the pastoral, more domestic emphasis.

Animal bone in particular blurs the line between artifacts and ecofacts since analysis of factors such as species, age, body parts, and butchering technique can suggest status and wealth differences between sites and suggest the degree of self-sufficiency or interdependence of households or settlements. Diana Crader (1984) analyzed faunal remains from two places at Thomas Jefferson's Monticello plantation in order to determine how status differences are reflected in food refuse. The storehouse was a small multipurpose building, and the dry well, or deep root cellar, was associated with the main house. The storehouse, situated along Mulberry Row, is suspected of having been used as a slave dwelling. There were less meaty cuts like crania, vertebrae, and ribs, probably prepared as stews, at the storehouse, and the occupants ate the occasional rabbit, opossum, squirrel, and game bird or chicken. Residents in the main house ate roasts of ham, pork, beef, mutton, and lamb. Crader compared the species that she identified with Jefferson's farm book, which indicates pork as the staple meat for both family and slaves. According to the archaeological remains, however, beef appears to have provided more meat for both the enslaved and the main household. An oral history by a longtime slave of Jefferson's reports that rabbits were raised, but that is not corroborated either by Jefferson's own records or by the archaeological assemblage.

Elizabeth Reitz (1994) examined faunal remains to gain insight into African foodways at Gracia Real de Santa Teresa de Mose near St. Augustine, Florida. Africans at this early to mid-eighteenth-century Spanish fort farmed their own lands and probably tended livestock as well as hunted, trapped, and fished. Domestic mammals were exclusively pig and cattle, but the low percentage of such domestic animals suggests a restricted access to this type of food. In comparing the African assemblage with those of a Native American mission settlement at Spanish St. Augustine, Reitz finds that each group had a different strategy. The Spanish had greater access to beef, pork, and poultry than did the Africans, while the Native Americans used no meat from European domestic animals. The Africans and Native Americans used a nearly identical range of estuarine resources, such as sharks, rays, and bony fishes.

The studies of New England's urban landscapes conducted by Mary Beaudry (e.g., Beaudry and Mrozowski 1988) and her colleagues combine data from palynology, plant macrofossils, zooarchaeology, archaeological features, and archival research to document historical changes that give a long-term perspective on the interaction between city dwellers and their environment.

Historical Features

In addition to artifacts and ecofacts, the nonportable archaeological features at a historical site are information containers. Historic site features might include building remains (e.g., concrete floors, foundations, building trenches, stockade post remnants), structures (e.g., mine headframes, concrete hoist pads, wells, privy pits, reservoirs), artifact concentrations (e.g., tin can dumps from boardinghouses, cyanide can lid dumps from cyanide mills, and glass bottle dumps from saloons), and landscape features (e.g., fence lines, ditches, footpaths, hedgerows, gardens, landforms such as mine waste rock dumps and mill tailings, cuts such as open pits, bulldozer cuts, and road cuts; railroad grades; canals). Historic features, however, seldom occur in isolation. Rather, they are parts of complexes or feature systems (Hardesty 1990) that reflect a technological or other activity complex such as a mill or mine.

Like all archaeological resources, features require a historic context in order to be interpreted. Before the Civil War, some residents of Slate Alley in Washington, D.C., dug a pit, measuring $5 \times 3 \times 1$ feet and filled it with 544 bottles of all types, some of which were identified as follows: 363 wine, 26 mineral water or beer, and 2 pharmaceutical with maker's marks from Philadelphia; Saratoga, New York; and Washington, D.C. Most of the bottles were whole. The contents of the pit also included hardware, window glass, bricks, marbles, nails, and faunal material. The archaeologists (Goodman et al. 1990) suggest that this pit was connected with junking, albeit an earlier than expected example. Junking was a full-time occupation for some alley men that supplemented the income of many families, particularly with the large population increase in the city during and after the Civil War. Junking involves "collecting of glass bottles and breaking them to be sold as broken glass by the hundreds of pounds; selling of old rags, paper, iron and tin, and any article of value which may be found among trash cans, or on the dumps. . . . Thus the disorder in the backyard was often the alley family's savings account and insurance policy" (Borchert 1982: 96).

Young boys junked, too. A Washington, D.C., housing reformer, writing in 1938, describes a nine-year-old Center Court boy who "gets up while the adults in the home are still in bed and with an axe (man's size) succeeds in breaking off enough kindling wood from the large boards taken from wrecked houses or from boxes found in the street, to start the fire in the kitchen stove." He "cuts school whenever possible and borrows a little wagon with which he collects junk and wood for his mother." Another nine-year-old in the same court " 'junks,' both working with his family and by himself, bringing in glass, paper, and rags" (cited in Borchert 1982: 144).

This local historic context can be connected to a much broader context, discussed by Mary and Adrian Praetzellis (1990). They report on the excavation of the Pioneer Junk Store in Sacramento, California, which revealed thousands of artifacts that may have been unsaleable discards from the secondhand store. The material included bottles and other glass, buttons, fabric, and metal. The consumerism of the late nineteenth and early twentieth centuries created at least two tiers of consumption. In addition to the cash trade for new goods by the upper and middle classes, there was demand for secondhand goods by middle- and working-class people (Praetzellis and Praetzellis 1990: 391). The mass market would have excluded whole segments of society were it not for the secondhand trade, which allowed cash-poor consumers to acquire higher-quality goods. Secondhand stores might have allowed barter in addition to cash sales. Junk stores were common in nineteenth- and early twentieth-century American cities, but trade in secondhand goods is not well documented in the written record (Praetzellis and Praetzellis 1990: 394). The archaeology of Samuel Stein's junk store along with documentary records "help us to understand the ethnic and economic strategies that enabled this immigrant merchant to adapt to life in 19th-century Sacramento" (Praetzellis and Praetzellis 1990: 399).

Archaeological Contexts

Archaeological information, finally, also comes from deposits and interfaces, or surfaces (fills, ditches, pits, trenches, water-deposited sediments, ash lenses) (Harris 1989). They provide information about fires, volcanic events, flood events, intentional burial episodes, historic land surfaces, and the like. Consider, for example, the archaeological record of Reipetown, Nevada, an early twentieth-century copper mining town (Hardesty 1998c). Artifact assemblages, aerial photographs, written accounts, and oral testimonies date the features to the time period between the 1890s and 1971. Aerial photographs taken in 1931, 1954, and 1971, for example, provide three time markers used to bracket the ages of buildings that can be identified and associated with archaeological features. Many of the excavated Reipetown features originate before the 1930s but have mostly secondary deposits originating in post-abandonment trash dumping or intentional filling of privy pits, wells, burned-out buildings, and the like between the late 1930s and the 1950s. Episodes of secondary deposition that are particularly important to understanding the formation of the Reipetown archaeological features are (1) the extension of water lines (1937) and sewer lines (1939) from the neighboring company town of Kimberly to Reipetown, followed by the filling in of wells and privy pits; (2) the Nevada Consolidated Copper Company's active removal of trash from Reipetown between 1934 and 1938 as part of a cleanup campaign; (3) major fires in 1908, 1917, and 1929 that leveled much of the town, followed by rebuilding upon house ruins after filling cellars with the burned debris and covering it over with new fill brought in from elsewhere; (4) the explosion of the town's population during the 1940s, with reoccupation of vacant houses and the construction of new housing by the Federal Housing Authority in 1943; and (5) mining companies' leveling off of the southwestern part of the townsite during and after World War II for truck and equipment parking.

ASSESSING THE INFORMATION CONTENT OF SITES

To determine what raw archaeological information a site actually contains, one should begin with documentary and ethnographic sources. Historic photographs, maps, and illustrations provide perhaps the most important documentary evidence of human activities that may be reflected in the archaeological record of a historic site. Town plats, for example, often provide important information about the geographical arrangement of human activities and how they changed in time and space. Thus, nineteenth-century miners coming from the eastern United States typically carried with them cultural concepts of settlements laid out in a grid pattern (Reps 1979). Consider, for example, the settlement of Shermantown, Nevada, that resulted from the Treasure Hill mining boom of the late 1860s (Hardesty 1999b). Major Edwin Sherman, a Civil War veteran and entrepreneur attracted to Nevada by earlier mining rushes, planned the settlement as a land development intended to "mine the pockets" of miners attracted to the Treasure Hill mines. He laid out the town to correspond with the image of a New England gridded town. Archaeological and documentary images of the evolution of the town, however, show that it developed along quite different lines, reflecting adaptations to local terrain and mining technology.

No information assessment of historical sites is complete without taking oral testimony into account. For twentieth-century sites, an important source of oral testimony are persons who once lived at a particular site or otherwise have intimate detailed personal knowledge of that site's past. Persons having artifact collections taken from a site or otherwise having information about that site's archaeological record are another source of ethnographic information.

The artifacts, features, and other material remains making up the historical site occur first and foremost in an archaeological context that defines the containers of archaeological information. Finding such containers and sampling their contents require a variety of field methods too numerous to describe in detail here, but which are familiar to archaeological practitioners. The techniques used to locate and assess the information value of historical sites include the use of historical maps and photographs, pedestrian surveys, and subsurface detection instruments (Orser and Fagan 1995: 126). Sanborn fire insurance maps, for example, provide detailed information about the location, size, construction characteristics, and uses of domestic, commercial, and industrial buildings and structures that once stood on many late nineteenth- and twentieth-century sites (e.g., Seasholes 1988: 106–7). Developing a good sampling strategy is critical to large-scale site surveys, because it is impossible to cover all of such areas on foot. Detailed site surveys of small samples of the area such as linear transects that have been selected carefully to be representative can be used to estimate site frequencies and types in the overall region (e.g., Thomas 1993). Geophysical prospecting is the most common method used to locate buried archaeological remains. Geophysical prospecting includes the use of such devices as metal detectors, proton magnetometers, ground-penetrating radar, sonar (for underwater detection), as well as methods such as electrical resistivity surveys and soil chemistry fingerprints (Orser and Fagan 1995: 126–39, see also, Clark 1990, Shapiro 1984, Weymouth 1986). Site information

assessment also includes recording of use and time-sensitive artifacts and features found on the site surface. More intrusive assessment methods include the use of backhoes, power augers, test
excavations, and shovel tests for probing buried deposits (e.g.,
Barker 1993, Deagan 1981). On-site field assessments such as these
provide some indication of the raw information content of a site.

WHAT MAKES ARCHAEOLOGICAL
INFORMATION IMPORTANT?

Criterion D requires making judgments about the relative value of
the archaeological information contained within historical sites.
How important is the information to scientific and scholarly research? Is it important enough to justify listing the site on the National Register of Historic Places? One consideration is whether the
site is a repository of descriptive and only minimally interpreted
information about the history of the modern world. In this sense,
most historical sites are information repositories that can be used to
answer future research questions that have yet to be asked. Answering the question of what is important, therefore, requires the development of strategies to preserve samples of the large variety of sites
containing the archaeological information needed to shed light on
future research questions (Hardesty 1995: 5). Preservation strategies
certainly include preserving samples of sites that represent categories of uninterpreted or middle-range information, such as large
and small sites, lakeshore sites, shipwrecks, townsites, and cyanide
mill sites. The argument for preservation of representative samples
has been made widely within the archaeological profession (e.g.,
Schaafsma 1989, Tainter and Lucas 1983: 716–17, McGimsey 1972,
Lipe 1974). The underlying, common concern is that archaeological
properties, like all historic properties, are limited and nonrenew-
able. Toward the goal of preserving a representative sample of sites,
assessing the information value of historical sites should take place
within the framework of local, state, and national sampling strategies aimed at preserving the past for the future.

Archaeology and other disciplines that glean important information from historic properties are evolving fields. Archaeological

techniques and methods have improved greatly even in the three decades since the passage of the National Historic Preservation Act. The questions that archaeologists ask have changed and become, in many cases, more detailed and more sophisticated. The history of archaeology is full of examples of important information being gleaned from sites previously thought to be unimportant. Sites that are now said to lack significance might, if they survive for another decade, be judged to have significance for their important information.

The other consideration—and the one that drives the current National Register interpretation of criterion D—is the importance of archaeological information to existing scientific and scholarly research. Assessing the information value of historical sites in this way requires the development of a research design. The research design defines the boundaries within which research takes place and lays out the assumptions, principles, and rules to be followed. Research designs include several steps.

- Identify what is to be explained.
- Identify the historic context and the explanatory framework within which research questioning takes place.
- Identify the important questions within the context.
- Stipulate the data needed to answer the important questions.
- Identify the methods to be used to assess the extent to which historical sites contain these data.

Context and Research Boundaries

Defining the boundaries of the ballpark within which research takes place is a critical first step to the development of a research design. The boundaries are geographical, temporal, and thematic. Both area of significance and historic context help define research boundaries for purposes of National Register evaluation. Consider, for example, how industry as an area of significance and industrial logging in the Lake Tahoe Basin, 1860–90, as a historic context define research boundaries. Archaeological information exists at different scales in time and space. Research into a regional mining community, for example, requires archaeological information on a regional scale, typically at the level of a mining district, and involves the study of regional settlement-systems. For this reason, defining research boundaries requires making a good logical connection between the geographical and temporal scale of archaeological information and the pattern of human behavior to be explained.

Research Objectives

Several objectives underlie the development of research designs. Particular questions tend to fall within the following objectives, which are the most common in historical archaeology.

- Preservation and Site Interpretation (Orser and Fagan 1995: 56). Management and public interpretation drive many research projects in historical archaeology. Much of the research is intended to gather information about how buildings and structures looked in the past. Hardesty (1997), for example, recovered archaeological data that allowed the reconstruction of one of the cabins at the site of one of the Donner Party's winter camps in the Sierra Nevada Mountains.
- Historical Supplementation (Deagan 1982, Little 1994a). Another common objective is creating ways of writing about the past that do not rely on historical documents or documentary historians as the final arbiters of meaningful or accurate history. Archaeology can supplement history by challenging traditional accounts. In a study of escape routes taken by the Northern Cheyenne during the 1879 outbreak from Fort Robinson, Nebraska, archaeological findings successfully challenged the official army-based accounts of the escape. Archaeology supported Cheyenne oral history (McDonald et al. 1991).
- Historical Ethnography (Deagan 1982, Little 1994a, Orser and Fagan 1995: 57; Schuyler 1988). Perhaps the most common goal is documenting the everyday lives of poorly documented people. Historical ethnography includes not only lifeways but also worldview (the cognitive dimension) and social/cultural processes such as ethnogenesis. Research goals in historical archaeology also include the comparative study of poorly documented social groups in the modern world, what Schuyler

(1988) calls historical ethnology. Documenting lifeways through historical archaeology is not just about the inarticulate or the disenfranchised. Archaeological ethnography must take into account the whole social system if we are to accurately interpret any part of it. John Otto (1984) examined status-related patterning in house sites, food remains, and artifacts at Cannon's Point Plantation (a sea-island plantation off the coast of Georgia) to see how status and access to surplus were reflected in the archaeological record. Three categories of occupants were planters, overseers, and slaves. Ceramic types were more alike between overseer and slave. Planters had more storage vessels, and their tableware was dominated by flatware serving pieces. In contrast, both overseers and slaves had more bowls, suggesting that they ate more soups and stews than they did roasts. About 25 percent of the overseer's ceramics were bowls, compared with 40 percent of the slaves'.

- Testing Ground for Archaeological Principles (Deagan 1982, Little 1994a). Another objective of research in historical archaeology is to more firmly ground explanatory principles in archaeology that can be used to interpret the more ancient past. In a classic example, James Deetz and Edwin Dethlefsen (1967) used data on changing styles of gravestone decoration in Colonial New England to study the validity of the long-used archaeological dating principle of seriation.

- Understanding modernization and globalization (Orser and Fagan 1995: 59; Little 1994a). Finally, the effort to understand the complex social and cultural processes of modernization and globalization drives many research projects in historical archaeology. Such an objective focuses on the global spread of material things, people, lifestyles, and ideas in the modern world; it also explores the worldwide contraction of space and time through economic, social, and cultural processes such as industrialization, capitalism, and rapid communication. Toward this end, Little (1994a) argues for an archaeology of capitalism concerns with (1) cross-cultural comparison, (2) production, consumption, and industrialism, and (3) ideology and power.

DEALING WITH REDUNDANCY

Without question, the most difficulty in assessing the information potential of a historical site comes from redundancy, the duplication of information from other sources. Other potential sources include documents, oral testimony, and other historical sites.

Documents and Oral Testimony

The availability of written records or oral testimony for site interpretation immediately opens up the issue of redundancy. Indeed, historians often question the usefulness of archaeological studies of historical sites for this very reason. Why excavate, they ask, when the answers to research questions can be found more cheaply and in much more detail in documents? The best response invokes richness, relevance, independence, and synergy.

Richness

Richness is one measure of archaeological significance. What about sites already documented in written accounts? The archaeological significance of historical sites often must be evaluated within the context of the richness of available information, written records, or other documentary materials.

In his book on the archaeology of Flowerdew Hundred Plantation in Virginia, James Deetz follows Marley Brown's (Colonial Williamsburg) concept of information loss in describing one approach to evaluating site significance. He asks (1993: 155):

> How much will we lose in information about its former occupants if we do not conduct excavations? If the amount is quite small, then the significance of the site is not all that great. On the other hand, the danger of losing a lot of knowledge by not excavating makes it more imperative that such a site be dug. What makes one site more liable to information loss than another is the degree to which it is represented in the documents. The less documentation, the more we stand to learn from excavation. Thus, site significance can be measured along two dimensions, time and documentary richness.

In this approach, the archaeological significance of a site increases not only as it becomes older but also as less is known about it from written accounts and other documents. The early seventeenth-century site of Wolstenholme Towne near Colonial Williamsburg in Virginia, for example, is highly significant because of the critical historical information about the first English settlements in Virginia that would have been lost if the site had not been excavated (Noel Hume 1982). In terms of richness, therefore, the most significant site in a region is the oldest and the least documented.

Relevance

Notwithstanding their richness, however, the relevance of documentary and oral testimony data as a source of information also must be considered. First and foremost, such information often provides the insiders' view of just a few literate people from a socially and politically dominant group that may or may not correspond with the grassroots data about actual behavior coming from archaeology. Second, the data may not be relevant to the most significant research questions. Thus, abundant documentary information about the philosophy and politics of an eighteenth-century family could be of limited value in answering research questions about, for example, consumer behavior or household organization or technology. In his introduction to the book *Historical Archaeology in Global Perspective*, James Deetz makes the case in a most compelling fashion (1991: 6):

> Archaeology certainly can provide insights into historical processes that written records simply do not provide. Historical archaeology deals with the unintended, the subconscious, the worldview, and mind-set of an individual. It provides access to the ways all people, not just a small group of literate people, organized their physical lives. If only the written records, rich and detailed as they are, are studied, then the conclusions will reflect only the story of a small minority of deviant, wealthy, white males, and little else. I do not think we want that for our national history; therefore, we need archaeologists to find what was left behind by everybody, for every conceivable reason. The unintentional record of people provides scholars with ways to determine the underlying reality of our history.

One example is the archaeological study of the sites of African-American households and settlements. Documentary accounts of these social groups often reflect racially based stereotypes and biases. In recent years, numerous archaeological studies have begun to shed more and better light on lifestyles and living conditions within both free and slave communities. They include studies of plantation slave settlements, such as William Kelso's work at Thomas Jefferson's Monticello in Virginia (1986), and free settlements, such as Kathleen Deagan's study of Gracia Real de Santa Teresa de Mose in Florida (Deagan and MacMahon 1995), and James Deetz's (1977) study of Parting Ways in New England.

Independence

But perhaps even more important than relevance is the issue of the independence of data acquired from the archaeological record, documents, and oral testimony. Rathje and Murphy's (1990) book *Rubbish! The Archaeology of Garbage* describes exactly this kind of problem. They collected information about foodways and other consumer behavior of domestic households in three ways: written questionnaires, oral interviews, and the study of trash cans and garbage dumps. Data about foodways in particular acquired from questionnaires and oral testimony differed quite dramatically from the grassroots observations taken from the archaeological record. Another example comes from the archaeological study of the site of Murphy's cabin, one of the cabins at Donner Lake in the Sierra Nevada Mountains of California, lived in by members of the Donner Party during the winter of 1846–47 (Hardesty 1997). Oral tradition considered the cabin to be the place where General Steven Watts Kearney's Mormon Battalion buried the remains of the Donner Party dead in June 1847. Archaeological excavation of the cabin site in 1984, however, failed to find any evidence of a mass grave.

Synergy

Finally, redundancy must be considered within the context of interplay between documents and archaeology that lead to synergies of interpretation, great leaps in understanding that would not be possible using either source of information about the past alone. The information content of historical sites lies not just in the archaeological record but in the interplay between the archaeological record, the documentary record, and other sources of information about the site. Images of the past come not only from written accounts and oral testimony but also from the material things contained in the architecture of surviving buildings, the archaeological record, and museum collections. Thus in his book *The Past Is a Foreign Country*, David Lowenthal argues that access to the past is gained by traveling along the routes of history, memory, and relics. But the routes, he observes, are best traversed in combination. "Each route requires the others for the journey to be significant and credible. Relics trigger recollection, which history affirms and extends backward in time. History in isolation is barren and lifeless; relics mean only what history and memory convey" (1985: 249).

Taking such material expressions into account, therefore, offers a richer, more comprehensive portrayal of the past.

There are at least five major ways that documentary and archaeological sources are used together in historical archaeology: contradictory, complementary, as sources for hypotheses, with information that is ripe for debunking, and when they are needed for context (Little 1992). In some cases, the data simply do not agree; sometimes oral history can weigh in when data contradict each other. The data could be played off each other in a middle-range theory approach. In many cases one data source addresses questions the other leaves out. Sometimes the sources can vary in trustworthiness and might be needed to bolster each other. Either data source may be used to debunk or rewrite some version of the past provided by the other. Hale Smith and John Griffin performed the first archaeology of Spanish missions in Florida in the 1940s. They also dismantled local identification of certain ruins as missions when archaeology revealed instead that they had been sugar mills and plantation buildings (Griffin 1994). Usually the documentary record provides a context for the interpretation of the archaeological record. We need to be extremely careful, however, in using historic contexts without allowing for the discovery of new or challenging information to arise from the archaeological record.

Perhaps the most important perspective needed to evaluate the significance of archaeological data from historical sites, however, is combining documents, archaeological data, and oral testimony in interactive models (Deetz 1988). In this approach, a beginning model or first approximation of community, household, or other social formation is developed from preliminary historical or archaeological research or both. The model then is used to identify hypotheses that can be tested with new documentary and archaeological data. Finally, the beginning model is revised to reflect the results of the new information, leading to yet other hypotheses that can be tested and further refinement of the model. The cyclical development of the model is typical of this strategy. In this way, the research strategy will develop in a series of phases in order to maximize the interpretive potential of data gathered in the field. Thus, the construction of history from the three sources of evidence is cyclical and continuously evolving.

Other Factors

The other issue of redundancy comes from the abundance and reliability of existing archaeological information that could be used to answer key research questions.

Age   The age of historical sites is another key issue. To be sure, the ages of historical sites are quite young in comparison with prehistoric sites. Age often is used as a significance criterion, as shown in the information loss concept from Flowerdew Hundred. Certainly the survivability of archaeological information tends to decrease with the increasing age of a site. Still, age often has nothing to do with the presence or absence of critical archaeological information needed to answer research questions. Historian William Robbins's book *Colony and Empire* (1994), for example, demonstrates that the late period between the 1890s and World War I marks the beginning of a major social and cultural transformation of the American West by industrial capitalism that continues throughout the twentieth century. Combined with documents and oral testimony, twentieth-century historical sites, therefore, should provide an enormous repository of archaeological information about the transformation. In addition, age is relative and must be placed in a regional context. For example, 150-year-old historical sites in the Great Basin, such as the Donner Party sites, are considered to be old; the same age of a historical site in New England is considered recent.

Time Span   Yet another key measure of significance is the length of time covered by the occupation of the property. Short-term and single-component sites provide the best information about some research questions or convey the best association with some historic themes. Most comparative studies require the time control best found in short-term sites. Single-component sites are best focused and, therefore, the most easily read or interpreted. Stratified sites provide the best information about social and cultural change over time. Such sites, therefore, are most significant for answering research questions involving change or for conveying an association with historic themes about change.

Uniqueness   In addition to age, documentary richness, and relevance, several other measures of archaeological significance should be considered. Perhaps the most obvious is the uniqueness of a historical site. The archaeological remains of the Donner Party's winter camps in the Sierra Nevada Mountains near Truckee, California, provide an illustration of a site that is highly significant because of its uniqueness (Hardesty 1997). In contrast, John Wilson (1990) shows that late historic farmstead sites are often considered, sometimes unfairly, not to be significant because "we've got thousands of these."

Visibility   Another measure of significance is visibility, which refers not just to the abundance of physical remains at a site but also to the ease of their discovery. At Fort Leonard Wood in Missouri, for example, Steven Smith (1994: 103) found that ground cover and wooded areas made the discovery of the archaeological remains of his hunter-squatter type of historic farmstead nearly impossible. If one were to be found, therefore, its significance would be high.

Survivability   Finally, survivability is another measure of the significance of historical sites. Consider, for example, the high likelihood that the archaeological remains of the earliest mining camps will be destroyed by later mining activity. Accordingly, the expected few surviving sites will have high significance.

CASE STUDY: EXAMINING WORLD SYSTEMS

The world-system paradigm, largely developed by historian Fernand Braudel and sociologist Immanuel Wallerstein in the 1960s and 1970s, focuses on the social and cultural processes of political economy to explain the origins and dynamics of the modern world. Underlying the approach is the concept of world system. A world system is a large-scale social system that can exist independently, that has a complex division of labor, and that is socially and culturally diverse (Sanderson and Hall 1995: 96). Historically, world systems are either (1) world empires, which are integrated by political or military force and are the most common, or (2) world economies, which are loose networks of economic production and exchange. Wallerstein argues that the emergence of a capitalistic world economy in sixteenth-century Europe created the first modern world systems. Others, however, see world economies emerging much earlier in China (e.g., Abu-Lughod 1989) or Mesopotamia (e.g., Frank and Gills 1993).

Big questions that count within the context of the world-system paradigm emerge from the general social and cultural processes that create and constantly change the structure of the capitalistic world economy. In Wallerstein's view, for example, the structure of the capitalistic world economy originates in relations of economic exchange. The growth of global markets and the resulting global division of labor led to the emergence of core, periphery, and semiperiphery regions with unequal or asymmetrical exchange relationships. Core regions are geographical centers of surplus accumulation and shifting seats of economic and political control of world systems. Peripheries, on the other hand, are marginal places/frontiers with the least surplus accumulation and the least economic and political control of world systems. The primary production and extraction of surplus takes place in peripheries. Semiperipheries, finally, are places somewhere between core and periphery.

Archaeologist Jack Williams (1992) gives an example of the use of archaeological data from the presidios in Arizona to test two competing hypotheses of the core-periphery relationships between Spain and New Spain. In one hypothesis, Wallerstein argues that New Spain has been a full-blown periphery of Spain since the sixteenth century. In the other, Fernand Braudel contends that New Spain and Spain enjoyed more or less equal relationships. Surplus accumulated in New Spain and transformed the Colonial economy. Bullion was extracted by private enterprise in New Spain, merchants in New Spain controlled the markets, and both accumulated surplus in the periphery. All that changed with the early nineteenth-century wars of liberation. The new republics established trade with industrial Britain, leading to Neocolonialism in Latin America that created a core-periphery relationship of the type described by Wallerstein.

How should one compare the two models with archaeological data? Wallerstein argues that essential goods reflect the unequal relationship between core and periphery. Essential goods are the things used in everyday life, such as tableware, food, and clothing. Peripheries have high percentages of essential goods coming from core regions. Williams (1992) notes the implications of essential goods for archaeological testing of the two models. Wallerstein's model would show high percentages of essential goods in New Spain after the sixteenth century. In contrast, Braudel's model would show high percentages of essential goods only after the Republic Period (1822–60) coming from Britain. Williams uses archaeological data from three presidios (military forts) in Arizona, dating between 1752 and 1856—Tubac, Tucson, and Santa Cruz—to test the two theories. Presidios housed the elite, who accumulated surplus in peripheries and, therefore, should best reflect trade and economic relations. Williams found that the percentage of essential goods coming from outside the region was low in the three presidios, suggesting that they were self-sufficient, and, therefore supporting Braudel's model. After 1860, however, increasing development of transportation, especially railroads, brought more essential goods from the core of the American world system, creating a true periphery.

CASE STUDY: POWER AND THE PLANTATION

Not everyone agrees, however, with Wallerstein's focus on the relations of exchange as the key to the structure of a world economy.

Eric Wolf, for example, argues that the relations of production are more important. The relations of production involve the social regulation of production and the distribution of labor, surplus, and wealth. The mode of production is the key concept, which Wolf (1982: 75) defines as "a specific historically occurring set of social relations through which labor is deployed to wrest energy from Nature by means of tools, skills, organization, and knowledge."

Unlike Wallerstein, who argues for a single capitalist mode of production operating and integrating diverse societies on a global scale after 1450, Wolf argues for many. In this view, world-system peripheries are hotbeds for the evolution of a wide variety of different modes of production, each some combination of capitalism, tributary, or kin-based production systems. All of these are linked together by capitalist relations of exchange and dominated by a capitalist global market.

One example of a distinctive mode of production that emerged in the modern world is the plantation. Comparative studies of how the plantation mode of production organized social relations is a key research area in historical archaeology. Charles Orser (1988), for example, uses power theory and focuses on conflict between socioeconomic classes as the key to understanding how archaeological remains are linked to the plantation mode of production. Orser defines two plantation classes: planters/owners and workers. One group produces surplus labor and the other extracts it.

The acquisition and distribution of material goods at archaeological sites on plantations reflect two sets of class relationships. First, the relationship between planters and slaves depends in part on the power structure in the South as a whole. The prestige of planters in the South was ranked by number of slaves and amount of land: a great planter had lots of slaves and land, a middle-class planter had twenty to forty slaves and one thousand acres, a small planter had ten to fifteen slaves and less than five hundred acres, and there were several farmer categories below this. Thus, slaves as a class served to indicate the planters' wealth/purchasing power. Therefore, archaeological evidence that the planter purchased ceramics for the slaves can be interpreted as a measure of power relationships with the outside world.

Another set of relationships between planter and slave classes is based on slaves as a source of labor and on the internal power structure of individual plantations. The power relationships between planters and slaves were quite different from the economic standing of the planter in Southern society. Within the plantation social field, planters and slaves worked out strategies of domination and resistance. The planters' domination strategy involved the use of force, withholding material goods and prestige jobs to discourage resistance, or giving of valued goods and prestige jobs to reward good work. Slaves could resist by "malingering, feigning ignorance, sabotaging machinery or tools, running away, or outright rebellion" (Orser 1988: 741). Two separate occupational hierarchies were based on power relationships within the slave class. One hierarchy was maintained by the owners, in which house slaves ranked highest and field slaves, lowest. Another hierarchy was maintained by the slaves. Here, slaves who could fool the master, heal the sick, preach, and care for the slave community ranked highest, and slaves who attended to the needs of the planter and family (house slaves) ranked lowest.

Charles Orser reanalyzed the artifact assemblages from Cannon's Point Plantation in Georgia and found that households of house slaves were much more like those of planters than those of field slaves. He found that planters gave house slaves special favors that included material culture. Field slaves, with a different view of the plantation social hierarchy, may have intentionally tried to distance themselves from the material culture of house slaves/planters by using distinctive boundary markers, such as different ceramic types (e.g., hand-painted decoration) and forms (e.g., bowls rather than plates).

WHAT'S NEXT?

The significance of historical sites as repositories of archaeological information clearly varies greatly from one site to another and requires the development of good research plans. Several chapters of part two are devoted to more detailed discussions of how to evaluate the significance and integrity of specific types of historical sites. They include linear sites (e.g., sites associated with transportation, communication, and power), industrial sites, domestic sites and farmsteads, and large-scale sites (e.g., townsites, plantations, and mining districts).

PART TWO

CASE STUDIES

4

Linear Sites

The archaeological record of the modern world is marked by linear sites and monuments associated with transportation, communication, and power networks. They include the remains of roads and trails, railroads, ships, shipwrecks, railroads, flumes, canals, telegraph lines, power lines, and pipelines. Aside from ships and shipwrecks, such sites typically are linear and present special problems in significance evaluation. There are two different ways that linear properties are likely to be nominated: as districts or as multiple property submissions. Linear resources are often treated as linear historic districts. A district refers to a concentration, linkage, or continuity of sites, buildings, structures, and objects that together represent an eligible entity. A historic district might contain properties that are individually eligible and at the same time contribute to the significance of the district. Within a historic district, individual resources are identified as contributing or noncontributing depending on historic associations, age, and integrity. It is not necessary to justify the individual importance of each component, because the significance of the district is based on the combined contribution of the individual elements.

Alterations to a piece of a larger district do not necessarily jeopardize the eligibility of the overall district. Continued repair and replacement of individual segments will not necessarily impair their ability to communicate historical significance. There is a point, however, at which a district will fail to contain enough remaining historic resources to convey a sense of historic time and place.

Replacement in kind or in comparable form might not destroy the contributing nature of the segments, but radical alterations could.

If a linear resource is not intact, but exists as noncontiguous bits and pieces across an extended area, then a multiple property submission (MPS) is appropriate. Listings of historic trails, for example, tend to be done as multiple property nominations because of integrity issues. That is, only extant portions of trails are normally listed, not the entire route, if there are missing segments. Individual properties along a linear corridor are evaluated in relation to a specific set of registration requirements that are laid out in a cover document that traces the historic development of the resources and provides a context for understanding the related properties. Registration requirements set specific standards for integrity and association. Each individual property nominated under the MPS cover document is evaluated for individual listing in the National Register.

The nomination must specify why the property is considered to be a significant resource and what essential physical features are necessary to illustrate that significance. Integrity must be related to the period of significance. If the resource retains the essential physical characteristics that defined it during its historic period of significance, it probably retains enough integrity to convey its significance. An eligible resource must be able to convey its historic identity, despite changes to certain elements.

BUILDING CONTEXT: DEFINING
SOCIOTECHNICAL SYSTEMS

Evaluating the significance of these sites begins by building an appropriate historic context. One approach is to define the context around the sociotechnical system of which transportation, communication, and power sites are a part. Timothy Nowak (1993), for example, evaluates the archaeological remains of the Union Pacific Railroad in Wyoming within the context of a transportation corridor system. The key parts of the system include railroad construction activities, railroad engineering and architecture, operation and maintenance activities, supply of fuel and other raw materials, and other railroad-related activities. Each of these subsystems is associated with property types. They include construction-related properties, industrial-related properties, operation and maintenance-related properties, and miscellaneous railroad-related properties. Construction property types are associated with the initial construction of the railroad. The most typical examples are survey camps, construction camps, tie hack camps, end of track towns, and military installations.

Industrial property types are associated with railroad engineering and supply. Railroad engineering properties include railroad grades, bridges, trestles, tunnels, landscape cuts and fills, snowsheds, and drains (e.g., culverts). Supply property types are associated with the raw materials and fuels used to construct, maintain, and operate the railroad. In this category are coal mines and facilities used to provide coal fuel for steam locomotives, sawmills, and other wood industry facilities used to supply ties for railroad construction and repair and for wood fuel for steam locomotives, and water tanks and conveyance systems for steam locomotives. Operation and maintenance property types are associated with the administrative organization, workforce, commercial activities, and day-to-day operation of the railroad. They include railroad towns, section houses for railroad maintenance crews, machine shops, roundhouses, coal yards, offices, supply depots, passenger depots, hotels, restaurants, division headquarters, water tanks, and pump houses. Miscellaneous railroad-related properties include the sites of railroad wrecks, railroad robberies, and commemorative monuments associated with the railroad.

Such sociotechnical systems are historically constituted and, therefore, have thematic, chronological, and geographical dimensions. Exploration properties, for example, typically are associated with the earliest time period in the development of a railroad. The next time period is associated with construction properties, followed by operation and maintenance properties and then by abandonment.

ASSESSING THE INFORMATION VALUE
OF HISTORIC TRAILS

What makes the information contained in transportation sites and monuments valuable? First of all, the information must have had or potentially have a significant impact upon the interpretation of important historical events or patterns, people, and architectural/engineering types associated with the trail. Secondly, the information must have cast, or have potential to cast, significant light upon important scientific or scholarly concepts, ideas, questions, hypotheses, theories, or models tied to important patterns and themes in local, state, or national history (after Hardesty 1999a).

Cultural Identity

The material expression of cultural identities might be important. Does the site or monument help interpret or provide significant information about historical events important to national cultural identities, such as ethnic groups or nationalities or social classes? The Mormon Pioneer National Historic Trail is a good example. Mormon history and cultural identity are associated with events taking place along the 1,300-mile trail, extending from Nauvoo, Illinois, to Salt Lake City, Utah, along which traveled the first Mormon immigrants to the American West. Another example is the Trail of Tears National Historic Trail, which consists of a water and overland corridor from Georgia and North Carolina to Oklahoma. The trail was used by the Cherokee Nation when it was forcefully removed from ancestral lands and is strongly associated with the history and cultural identity of the Cherokee.

There are many other trail properties listed on the National Register. Many are segments of migration routes, such as the Santa Fe Trail, Oregon Trail, Whoop-Up Trail, Applegate-Lassen Trail, and Bozeman Trail. Some trails listed for their significance in the movement primarily of European Americans were Indian trails before. The Lolo Trail, for example, is a National Historic Landmark in Idaho and Montana because it was the most arduous single stretch of Lewis and Clark's trek. Prior to that, it was a Nez Percé route to the plains for buffalo hunting.

The Evolution of Political Economy

Historic trails might contain information that helps interpret or provide significant information about economic or political developments that are important in local, state, or national history. To what extent, for example, were stage stations or railroad towns or river towns along waterways or overland trails or roads social and economic central places in the region? Is there, for example, evidence of nucleated settlements around the stations? Are way stations centers of economic distribution for the region? Transportation sites and monuments might contain information about the economic and political peripheralization of regions. Overland transportation networks, for example, are the vanguard of world systems expanding into and incorporating peripheral regions (Hall 1989, Wallerstein 1974, Williams 1992). As nodes of settlement and population in frontier transportation networks, trails not only reflect but also play a part in the process of incorporation.

Demography

Historic trails might contain significant information about migrations and other historically important demographic events and processes in local, state, and national population history. Historically important migrations in the nation's history, for example, include several mining rushes to precious metal discoveries such as the California gold rush. Each of the rushes is associated with trails, roads, and waterways carrying people and materials and for this reason has national importance. The material expression of these historic routes often includes archaeological and other material remains that contain significant information capable of helping to interpret and to answer important scholarly and scientific questions about the mining rushes.

Environmental Change

Historic trails might contain information about the formation of landscapes or episodes of environmental change that are significant in local, state, or national history. Key landscape elements containing this information include (1) the evolution of settlement patterns associated with the route (e.g., changes in the type and arrangement of such settlements as entrepôts, primary way stations such as home stations, railroad towns, or river towns); (2) the evolution of vegetation patterns associated with the route (e.g., deforestation brought about by timber cutting for steam locomotive fuel along railroads. Information about such changes by using pollen profiles, dendrochronology, etc.); (3) the evolution of landforms associated with transportation routes; and (4) the evolution of ethnic and other cultural landscapes expressing cultural identities associated with the routes.

The Evolution of Technology

Finally, historic trails might help interpret or provide significant information about technological innovations, transfers, types, and patterns important in the history of technology. The engineering of trails, roads, railroads, and canals through rugged mountainous terrain, for example, often involved technological innovations and transfers that became national and global standards.

CASE STUDY: PORTAGE TRAILS IN MINNESOTA

Robert Vogel and David Stanley (1991) developed two historic contexts for the MPS "Portage Trails in Minnesota, 1630s–1870s." The contact period from the 1630s to 1837 is associated with Eastern Dakota, Ojibwa, French, British, and U.S. trade. The post-contact period from 1837 to the 1930s is associated with Indian communities and reservations. Portage trails were an important link in water transportation systems, whereby boats and their cargo were carried overland when water travel was interrupted by rapids, falls, or shallow if the water routes weren't connected. Such trails were created and used by Native Americans and were essential to the fur trade. The fur trade is a dominant theme in all of the contact period contexts. It shaped Minnesota's economy and had great impact on Native American cultures, which traded with the French (mid-1600s to 1763), English (1763–1803), and Americans (1803–c.1850). Beaver were taken in winter when pelts were prime. European traders and Native middlemen collected furs at wintering posts near villages, packed for transport, and, after the ice broke, shipped trade goods from Montreal or St. Louis to depots on the periphery of the fur trade area, along Lake Superior and the Mississippi River, where each spring traders rendezvoused to pick up goods and head for interior trading posts.

The MPS treats portage trails, relicts of a once-dominant landscape form, as archaeological sites and as vernacular or cultural landscapes. The single property type identified in the MPS is the portage trail. This property type includes high and low portage trailways, canoe drags, terminals and landings, poses, bivouacs, caches, and canoe repair sites. Low portage trails follow the shortest and most direct routes, which were usually narrow, undulating, marshy, or boggy. High portage trails followed overland routes that were detours around obstructions. Over time, these became rutted and sunken and were sometimes marked. Terminals or landings marked the beginnings and ends of trails. A few acquired permanent trading posts or forts, but more often had intermittent stores. A pose, or pause or post, is a canoe or pack rest along a trail. A cache contained objects stored for future use. Trails that are historic landscapes are entrenched as much as one to two feet and might be associated with a particular vegetation complex. Associated vegetation might consist of disturbed upland and riverine plants and be marked by selective thinning and topsoil disturbance. For example, galleries of bottomland trees might extend into pine-covered uplands. Relict portage trails are vernacular transportation structures that might be eligible under criterion A for their association with the transportation geography of Minnesota and represent diverse themes such as internal transportation networks, the pelt trade, and the impact of birch bark canoe on mobility. Under criterion C a relict trail represents a vernacular type of cultural landscape, that is, cultural landforms shaped by historical and natural processes.

In Minnesota, portages are as important as roads, oxcart trails, stage routes, and other transportation properties. Research questions associated with trails include: Do portage trails predate European contact, and how old are they? When were specific regions opened to fur trade? How did the material culture of the voyageur change over time?

Artifacts might be in a secondary archaeological context because of erosion, logging, or agriculture, but the general location of diagnostic artifacts might well contribute important information. As an individual nomination under this MPS, the Height of Land Portage in St. Louis County is listed under criteria A and D for archaeology, exploration/settlement, and transportation. It is a network of portage trails and waterways connecting the Embarrass River with the Pike River and Vermilion Lake and includes high and low trails, poses, and probably bivouacs. The property consists of two discontiguous trail segments along 4.6 miles. The segments convey a sense of landscape cohesiveness through location, setting, and association. Archaeological features likely to be associated include trail surfaces, linear scatters of artifacts, artifact scatters, hearths, structures associated with poses, bivouacs, caches, and portage landings.

CASE STUDY: ASSESSING WATER CONVEYANCE SYSTEMS

Dana Supernowicz (1990) developed eligibility criteria for historic water conveyance systems in the El Dorado National Forest. The basic features of the systems, such as ditches, canals, flumes, pipes, and penstocks, carry water for a variety of purposes (e.g., mining, logging, irrigation, and hydroelectric power). In addition, the water conveyance systems have many other features that are associated with their engineering, maintenance, and operation. They include retaining walls, roads, ponds, work camps or households, dams, and tunnels. Criteria for assessing the eligibility of the physical remains of water conveyance systems include size, length, and integrity. Supernowicz classifies ditches and canals, for example, into three size and length categories, ranging from large to small. Thus, large ditches and canals are defined as a mile or more in length, three feet or more in depth, and five feet or more in width. In addition, he classifies ditches, canals, and associated features into integrity categories based on how much of their original use and design is still intact. The best integrity category, for example, includes such characteristics as: (1) no recent alterations or significant erosion; (2) earthen ditches still retain their original morphology, profile, and design elements; and (3) retains features associated with either the design or original function of the system, and those features retain their original form and appearance.

The worst integrity category involves more than 50 percent alteration and the loss of all associated features. Finally, the water conveyance system, now classified by size, length, and integrity, is evaluated within its historic context and period of significance.

CASE STUDY: RAILROAD LOGGING IN ARIZONA

Pat Stein (1995) developed the context, "Railroad Logging on the Coconino and Kaibab National Forests, 1887 to 1966," as part of an MPS on logging railroad resources in those forests in Arizona. Although the study area of more than 1.4 million acres has not been fully surveyed, eight property types associated with railroad logging have been defined along with the criteria under which they are likely to be eligible. Other property types, such as train wrecks, might be present in the study area but have not yet been identified. Because the impact of railroad logging was felt most keenly at the local level, the local level of significance is recommended for most of the properties identified.

Rolling Stock

Rolling stock refers to the wheeled vehicles such as locomotives and log carrier cars that are used on railroad grades. These vehicles might be eligible under criterion C, because they embody the distinctive design characteristics of a technology. Under criterion A, they evoke the industry that made significant contributions to local history. To be eligible within the historic context, the stock must (1) have been used in the study area so that integrity of association is retained, (2) be located in the study area so that integrity of setting is retained, and (3) retain its distinctive characteristics so that integrity of design and workmanship are retained.

Railroad Grades

Railroad grades are the roadbed foundations that allowed movement of rolling stock. These grades include main lines, spurs, sidings, and wyes. Main lines provided access to the general cutting areas. Spurs branched off the main line for access to particular cutting units. Sidings were short segments of double track that permitted trains to pass one another. Wyes were y-shaped tracks that permitted trains to reverse direction by heading up one arm and backing down the other. In most cases, grades were constructed by depositing ballast of crushed rock or earth to prepare a level, dry base for the ties, which were often of untreated pine. Some grades were cut into slopes instead. After use, rails were usually removed and ties were often salvaged by local residents for reuse. Roads for logging trucks were often built on the railroad grades.

   To be eligible in this context and retain integrity of association, the grade must have been used as part of a logging railroad and not for another purpose such as mining. Grades are strong visual clues to the enormous logging industry. To be eligible under criterion A, they must contain sections that convey a visual sense of the logging lifeline connecting wilderness and civilization. The section of grade must have a majority of its ties in place or a majority of its bed intact. The section of grade must provide a line of sight that carries the viewer's eye a substantial distance through the forest. In some cases, the grades might be well preserved enough to convey the design and workmanship of the method of construction to be eligible under criterion C.

Inclines

Inclines are cable-operated railroads built on the side of a hill. These were built to lower loaded cars down grades that were too steep for locomotives. Inclines allowed harvesting of timber from nearly inaccessible areas. Because of their highly specialized design characteristics, they might be eligible under criterion C, if integrity of association, design, and workmanship are present. More than half of the incline's slope must be intact so that the basic design characteristics are apparent.

Rural Historic Landscape

A rural historic landscape is a landscape that reflects the daily work of railroad logging. Such landscapes are not designed but evolve in response to natural and economic forces. One type of rural historic landscape associated with logging is the clear-cut. Prior to 1910, clear-cutting was done manually, leaving knee- to waist-high stumps. After 1910, Forest Service regulations took effect that prohibited such intensive harvesting, replacing the practice of clear-cutting with the principle of sustained yield. Clear-cut areas with high stumps evoke the intensive cutting of thriving railroad logging and might be eligible because of their strong association with the historic context under criterion A. To be eligible, the landscape must be associated with railroad logging. Clear-cutting was practiced even before the establishment of logging railroads. If a railroad grade is within one-half mile of the clear-cut landscape property, it is safe to assume an association with the railroad-logging context. The clear-cut must convey a sense of large-scale, intensive tree harvesting.

Big Wheels

Big wheels are two-wheeled, single-axle carts that were used until the late 1920s for skidding logs to the railroads. Logs were first bunched into transportable piles. A teamster then would back the big wheel over the pile and attach the logs beneath the axle of the cart. With the load suspended in this way, the wheels rather than the draft animals bore most of the load. Big wheels represent a technological solution to the problem of transporting big loads without mechanization and, therefore, might be eligible under criterion C. Under criterion A, big wheels symbolize old logging practices and evoke the era when Flagstaff and Williams were simply logging towns. To retain integrity of association and setting, a big wheel cart must have been used within the study area during the era of railroad logging and still be located within the area or have been returned to it. In addition, the property must be intact enough to convey to a viewer how it looked and functioned. Both of its wheels should be upright and attached to the axle to retain integrity of design.

Sawmills

Sawmills were mechanical facilities for reducing logs to lumber. There were both large, permanent mills and small sawmills. Large mills, capable of producing 100 thousand board feet per day, were situated where the lumber companies connected with the transcontinental railway. Small mills, which could produce up to ten thousand board feet per day, were erected for specific tasks and moved or shut down as the tasks were completed. Small mills tended to be located in the backwoods. Often they provided ties for logging railroads. Within the study area, historic sawmills exist as archaeological sites. Some of these might help to provide a detailed understanding of the material culture of the lumber industry in northern Arizona and, therefore, might be eligible under criterion D if integrity of association and materials are present. The property must have functioned as part of a logging railroad system. If there is no railroad grade within one-half mile of the site, an association with this context is unlikely. If the surface has been disturbed, there must be intact subsurface remains that are likely to yield significant information.

Logging Camps

Logging camps are work stations for tending laborers, livestock, and equipment needed for logging activities. They provided food and shelter for both workers and animals and were used to tend the pigs, chickens, and other animals that supplemented the workers' diet. Minor repairs were made on logging equipment, and draft animals were shoed at logging camps. Camps were situated close to the area being cut and moved as soon as the work was finished. By the 1920s, logging companies were using portable camps that could be loaded onto rail cars to move to a new area. Within the study area, there are at least 102 logging camps recorded as archaeological sites. Features include cabins, mess halls, camp kitchens, blacksmith forges, scalers' cabins, commissaries, privies, boardwalks, corrals, sleds, and other features and equipment. Archaeological investigation of logging camps could address important research questions, such as (1) Did some camps serve specialized functions? (2) Were camps segregated by ethnic group? (3) When did families reside at camps, and how did the presence of families affect the operation of the camps? (4) What were the sanitary and health conditions in camps? (5) How did camps change through time? and (6)

How did camps of different logging companies differ? To be eligible, camps must have been associated with railroad logging. Isolated trash is not eligible in this historic context. The sites must contain surface or subsurface remains capable of yielding important information. A site with good visibility and good focus will likely be eligible, while a site with neither good visibility nor good focus likely will not be eligible. A site with poor visibility and good focus might be eligible if the data are relevant to a carefully framed research question. A site with good visibility and poor focus is not likely to be eligible.

Trestles

Trestles are structures that cross streams, drainages, and depressions. Logging companies built trestles to provide the gentlest possible grade for their railroads. They were technological solutions to irregular topography and allowed trains to pass through rugged terrain. Trestles are significant for their method and type of construction and, therefore, might be eligible under criterion C. Where grades have been obliterated, trestles might provide the only information about the location of logging railroads and, therefore, could be eligible under criterion D, if integrity of association, design, and workmanship are present.

Summary

Historical archaeologists often encounter the archaeological remains of railroads. How to evaluate the significance and integrity of railroads as linear sites is illustrated by the Coconino and Kaibab National Forest example. The most important property types associated with the historic context developed for the railroads are rolling stock, railroad grades, inclines, rural historic landscapes, big wheels, sawmills, logging camps, and trestles. Identification of the most important significance criteria is the first step to evaluating the National Register eligibility of examples of each property type. Rural historic landscapes, for example, are best evaluated for significance under criterion A, sawmills and logging camps, under

criterion D, and inclines, under criterion C. The integrity requirements of each property type also varies.

CASE STUDY: THE HENNESS PASS ROAD

The Henness Pass Road through the Sierra Nevada Mountains in
California and Nevada is an example of an overland road system
first used as part of the California Trail and then developed into a
toll road servicing the Gold Rush and Comstock mines and settlements (Hardesty et al. 1997). The historic context for the Henness
Pass Road spans the time period from 1845 to 1880 and is associated
with the themes of overland emigration on the California Trail
(1845–48), the California gold rush (1849–58), and mining on the
Comstock Lode (1859–67). The archaeological remains and other
historic properties associated with the Henness Pass Road are
linked to its historic context with property types. Important property types include emigrant campsites, caches, graves, way stations,
and road engineering properties, such as roadbeds, bridges, tunnels, and culverts.

Caches

Cache sites are the remains of buried or otherwise stored goods left
behind by overland emigrants, a common practice along the California Trail. Cache sites include open pits where goods have been
removed and surface depressions marking undisturbed caches.
Under criterion A, cache sites might be eligible for the National
Register because of their strong association with overland emigration. To be eligible, however, the properties must have sufficient visibility to convey the association and retain integrity of location, association, and setting. Even if determined to be ineligible by
themselves, cache sites might also contribute to the eligibility of a
roadbed segment under criterion A if they enhance the association
between the roadbed and overland emigration. In addition, the
cache sites could be eligible under criterion D. Key research questions for evaluating the information value of caches include the nature of the baggage carried by overland emigrants, what goods

were considered more expendable than others, and the evolution of consumerism in America. The properties must retain integrity of association, workmanship, and materials to be eligible under criterion D.

Graves

The occasional death of travelers on the Henness Pass Road could have led to burial by the roadside. Graves as a property type include grave markers, rock cairns, human remains or grave goods, fenced or otherwise protected areas, and cemetery plots. Graves are not usually considered to be eligible for the National Register by themselves, however, graves might contribute to the eligibility of a roadbed segment under criterion A if they enhance the association between the roadbed and overland emigration. To be eligible, the properties must have sufficient visibility to convey the association and retain integrity of location, design, association, and setting. In addition, graves could be eligible under criterion D. Key research issues for evaluating the information value of graves include demography, disease and accident patterns, ideology and mind-set, artifact consumption patterns, and social status, such as gender and ethnicity. To be eligible under criterion D, graves must retain integrity of association.

Emigrant Camps

This property type is strongly associated with overland emigration. After leaving the Truckee River at Verdi, overland emigrants traveling on the California Trail climbed a steep grade and then descended into Dog Valley, where they camped for a short time. The emigrant campsite property type is defined by a geographically localized scatter of artifacts dating to the overland emigration period. Most of the artifacts should reflect foodways, transportation, and personal adornment, clothing, and lifestyle. Emigrant campsites are likely to have few material remains and would not normally be eligible under criterion A. The more visible examples of the property type, however, could be contributing if they enhance the association between a roadbed remnant and the overland emigration context. To be eligible under criterion A, campsites should retain integrity of location, setting, and association. Temporary campsites are more likely to be eligible under criterion D for their information value. Key research questions for judging the information value of the campsites would focus on the social and cultural characteristics of the travelers (such as class, origin, ethnicity, and gender) and on the characteristics of campsite location. To be eligible under criterion D, campsites should retain integrity of association, design, and materials.

Way Stations

The Henness Pass Road was dotted with way stations to maintain staging and freighting traffic during the gold rush and Comstock periods. Way stations supplied livestock maintenance, equipment maintenance, and hostelry services to travelers along the road. In addition, some way stations served as toll houses during the Comstock period when the Henness Pass Road operated as a toll road. Finally, some way stations were resorts (e.g., Webber's Hotel) and working ranches as well, working under contract with staging and freighting companies. The characteristics of way stations as a property type typically include a residence, outbuildings, corral, and well.

Way stations might be eligible for their association with the gold rush or Comstock periods under criterion A or for their association with an important person under criterion B. Location, setting, and association are the key elements of integrity; way station properties must be highly visible to retain integrity. In addition, they might be eligible under criterion C as an expression of a distinctive technological pattern. To be eligible in this case, they need to retain integrity of materials, workmanship, and design. Under criterion D, they might be eligible for their information value. Key research issues include way stations as commercial households, world-system relationships, consumerism, technology, and social structure (e.g., gender, class, and ethnic relations). To be eligible under criterion D, way station properties should retain integrity of location, design, and association.

Road Engineering Features

Road engineering features make up another important property type associated with the Henness Pass Road historic context. Although not much more than an unimproved wagon road in its early years, the road underwent major improvements during the Comstock period. Still, however, the improvements were too early for the use of early mechanized equipment and, therefore, would have involved hand tools. Not until the 1870s, for example, was the horse-drawn elevating grader introduced. David Byrd's (1992: 15) characterization of the improved road, therefore, as "15 to 18 feet wide, banked, outfitted with ditches for drainage and the elevation was no more than six feet to the hundred," probably is the best description of the roadbed remnants of the Henness Pass Road. Bridges, tunnels, culverts, cut and fill landscape features, and other engineering features are also included within this property type. Continued use of some sections of the road to the present day, however, suggest that many of the most visible engineering features, especially existing bridges, date after the period of significance and, therefore, are not associated with the historic context.

Some roadbed remnants of the Henness Pass Road could be eligible for the National Register under criterion A for their association with the overland emigration period. Integrity is a key issue. To be eligible, the road segment should retain the visual appearance of a primitive road. Stephen Beckham and Richard Hanes (1991), for example, considered feeling, location, design, setting, association, and materials to be important elements of integrity in evaluating the eligibility of segments of the Barlow Road, a segment of the Oregon Trail in Clackamas County, Oregon. Thus, the feeling and setting of a primitive road should be rural, the location of the road should be confirmed through historic documentation, the design of the road should reflect its use as a wagon road (e.g., wagon width), the road segment should be sufficiently intact to convey its association with overland emigration, and the materials used in construction should be indigenous.

In addition, roadbed remnants and other engineering features could be eligible under criterion C as examples of a pattern of road engineering technology. To be eligible in this case, they need to retain integrity of materials, workmanship, and design. Finally, roadbed remnants could be eligible under criterion D for their information value. Key research issues needed to determine information value focus on road engineering methods, the evolution of transportation, the evolution of regional settlement systems, and road capitalization (Beckham and Hanes 1991). Under criterion D, the roadbed must retain integrity of association, materials, and workmanship.

Summary

Overland roads and trails are among the most common modern world remains likely to be encountered by historical archaeologists. They often have long histories and, therefore, could be associated with multiple time periods, historical themes, geographical boundaries, and property types. The physical characteristics of overland roads might change over time as a reflection of new uses and the evolution of technology. Evaluating the significance and integrity of the remains of historic roads and trails must take all of this into consideration. The Henness Pass Road provides a typical example. Caches, graves, emigrant camps, way stations, and road engineering features are the most important property types associated with the road's historic context. Examples of each property type could contribute to the overall significance of the Henness Pass Road or could be individually eligible for listing on the National Register. The following chapter discusses how to evaluate the archaeological significance and integrity of industrial sites, another major site type likely to be encountered by archaeologists working with the archaeological record of the modern world.

5

Industrial Sites and Monuments

New patterns of commerce and industry define the modern world. Not surprisingly, therefore, the archaeological remains of modern world industries are often abundant and important (Gordon and Malone 1994, Palmer and Neaverson 1998). They include the remains of the technologies and workplaces of extractive industries, such as mining and logging, manufacturing, transportation, agriculture and food processing, power, and communication systems. They also include the remains of residential sites and other domestic activities, such as boardinghouses, work camps, and company towns. And they include industrial landscapes.

Wilbert Moore (1965) defines industry in the most general sense as the transformation of raw materials into intermediate components or finished products by primarily mechanical means using an inanimate source of power. Industry is best viewed as a total system that includes raw materials, tools, operational sequences and skills, social and cultural knowledge, work coordination, and the historical context within which these parts and their interactions occur (Pfaffenberger 1992: 497).

Evaluating the significance of an industrial site begins with the development of historic contexts and research designs and ends with on-site assessment of integrity, information value, and interpretive value. Several themes are especially useful in the development of historic contexts for industrial properties. They include labor history, labor economics, social history, history of science and technology, environmental history, ethnic history, industrial society and culture, and globalization.

DEFINING INDUSTRIAL PROPERTY TYPES

The key to evaluating industrial sites and monuments is the property type, the most direct link between a historic context and the archaeological remains of an industry. Industrial property types most often are associated with technologies, social formations and cultures, and landscapes. Consider, for example, the property types associated with the wood industry in the Lake Tahoe Basin of California and Nevada during the Comstock era (Lindstrom and Hall 1994). "The Wood Industry in the Lake Tahoe Basin, California and Nevada, 1859–1890" defines the historic context. The property types associated with the historic context fall into the following categories:

Wood harvesting properties are associated with the activities of wood cutting and stacking. They include wood felling stations and wood yards.

Wood conveyance property types include animal conveyance systems, railroad conveyance systems, gravity conveyance systems, and water conveyance systems. The Great Incline of the Sierra Nevada, a funicular or cable railroad that transported cordwood and lumber from sawmills in the basin to flumes in the mountains above the lake, is a good example of a property type in this category.

The conveyance systems brought the harvested trees to sawmills or to more specialized wood processing stations such as shingle mills, box and planing mills, or charcoal kilns or pits.

The engineer-designed lumbering complex property type is an integrated system of wood harvesting sites, mills, transportation networks, power houses, worker's housing, company store, administrative office, and other facilities.

The isolated worker's housing property type consists of log cabins that housed most workers in the industry. Some workers also lived in wood frame cabins, dugouts, and stone cabins.

The work camp property type consists of small work camps, such as woodcutters' camps, flume tenders camps, and tallow stations for greasing flumes. Large work camps served as centralized collection places and staging areas.

In addition to work camps, the Comstock wood industry supported towns in the Lake Tahoe Basin. Glenbrook and other small industrial towns in the basin appear to be situated on the shores of Lake Tahoe.

Finally, the Lake Tahoe Basin also includes a variety of landscapes that have been transformed in a distinctive way by the wood industry. Typical industrial landscapes include the remnants of clear-cut forests containing cut stumps dating to the period but now overgrown with secondary forests.

LINKING ARCHAEOLOGICAL RESOURCES TO PROPERTY TYPES

The archaeological record of industrialism, however, typically consists not of well-preserved property types that can be easily linked to historic contexts but of their disconnected remnants. Such archaeological resource types include building foundations, privy pits, wells, mine waste rock dumps, cordwood piles, ditches, slag dumps, pottery waste piles, and the like. But archaeological resource types must be linked together into property types to effectively take advantage of the historic context as a tool for evaluation.

The concept of feature system, discussed previously, facilitates the process. Industrial households, for example, typically are visible in the archaeological record as a geographical cluster of domestic features that might include a building foundation or a leveled-off terrace where a building or a tent once stood, a privy pit, possibly a well, a footpath, and a scatter of domestic trash. The material expression of the household, however, is often warped by overlays of the remains of industrial technologies or later nondomestic activities. Developing a model of a domestic household feature system makes it possible to separate the archaeological image of the household property type from the other images.

The same approach is used to define industrial technology feature systems. Consider, for example, the blast furnaces used in some iron making industries. Blast furnaces, unlike bloomery furnaces, create temperatures high enough to melt iron. They are tall chimney-like structures with a hearth at the base. Iron makers pour

a charge of crushed iron ore, coke, or charcoal for fuel and limestone or oyster shell as a flux into the top of the furnace. Blast furnaces use a blast of air introduced through tuyeres (nozzles into the
hearth to induce burning). (Initially water power and later steam
engines were used to create the air blast.) The melted charge then
flows either into trenches, called pigs, or directly into molds (e.g.,
for cannon balls, kettles, or bells), and slag is skimmed off the top.
The site of the 1860s Bluff Furnace in Chattanooga, Tennessee, illustrates the typical archaeological remains of a blast furnace (Council
et al. 1992: 98). Distinctive archaeological features include the remains of the casting shed, the charging deck, the boiler/smokestack
foundation, the steam engine mounts, and the bases of the furnace.
Later archaeological features not associated with the Bluff Furnace,
and therefore not part of the blast furnace feature system, include
retaining walls, drainage system, and the foundation of a domestic
building.

ASSESSING THE HISTORICAL VALUE
OF INDUSTRIAL SITES

Industrial sites and monuments could have many values within the
historical context developed for purposes of significance evaluation. Certainly well-preserved sites often are valuable as surviving
examples of historically important industrial technologies, workplaces, architecture, settlements, and landscapes. They might illustrate or convey to present-day observers significant historical
events, themes, cultural identities, architectural or engineering
types or styles, or people and, therefore, be eligible under National
Register criteria A, B, or C. But the information content (criterion
D) of industrial sites is perhaps the most common, and at the same
time the most difficult, historical value to assess.

Assessing the information value of an industrial site or monument begins with the development of a research design that clearly
defines the research questions to be answered by information contained in the material remains of the industry represented. Consider, for example, one general research question that might be
used to guide the evaluation of the archaeological remains of the

wood industry in the Lake Tahoe Basin discussed previously. Extractive industries such as lumbering in the Lake Tahoe Basin reflect the global expansion of capitalistic world systems. The global patterns of capitalistic society and culture, however, are not monolithic; they reflect regional differences in environment, history, and indigenous peoples. The Lake Tahoe Basin forms one such region as an extractive frontier or periphery of capitalistic world systems in the nineteenth and twentieth centuries. Wood industry properties within the Lake Tahoe Basin potentially contain information about the regional expression of a distinctive social formation and culture of capitalism.

The information contained in an industrial site comes from a variety of sources. One source is the remains of buildings, structures, machines, or other objects. Such industrial architecture often contains information about architectural design, engineering, and construction methods. It also might include information about the functions, uses, and meanings of buildings and structures (e.g., machinery and workplace layout, symbolism). The interpretation of the remains of industrial buildings and structures is often facilitated by the use of documents (e.g., company records, pictorials, maps, technical books, and journals), oral testimony, and experimental archaeology. Archaeologists at Old Sturbridge Village in Massachusetts, for example, interpreted the pottery-making technology used there in the early nineteenth century, using information gathered from the construction and operation of an experimental kiln (Worrell 1985).

The physical analysis of artifacts from industrial sites is another source of information. Robert Gordon and Patrick Malone (1994: 24–32), for example, discuss the use of archaeometry for this purpose. Archaeometry involves the physical examination of artifacts, using engineering analysis, materials research, and surface markings. Engineering analysis applies engineering principles to interpretation. Gordon and Malone (1994: 24), for example, found that "measurements of the sizes and shapes of lock parts from military small arms show that the precision attained by American armory artisans in hand-filing . . . improved tenfold between 1810 and 1850." Analyzing the physical structure and composition of industrial artifacts through such methods as electron and optical microscopy and trace element analysis often shows how an artifact was made and used. Wear patterns and other surface markings also show how an artifact was made or used. Thus, Edwin Battison (1966) used surface markings to show that the lock mechanisms of a musket made at Eli Whitney's armory could not have been made with machine-milled parts.

EVALUATING INDUSTRIAL TECHNOLOGY SITES

Perhaps the most common type of industrial site is associated with industrial technology. The sites of industrial technologies tend to fall into one of the following categories or patterns:

Extractive industries (e.g., mining, logging, evaporative salt works)

Manufacturing (e.g., pottery kilns, armories, iron making, textile mills, glassworks)

Transportation (e.g., turnpikes and toll roads, canals, steamboats, railroads, automobiles, and air transport facilities)

Agriculture and food processing (e.g., ranching, irrigation farming, canning plants, fisheries)

Power (e.g., steam engines, hydroelectric plants, windmills, wind generators, water power plants)

Communications (e.g., telegraph, telephone)

Scale and Boundaries

Perhaps the most critical step in evaluating the archaeological remains of industrial technologies is finding the appropriate geographical scale. Industrial technologies typically occur on a large geographical scale and have complex and diverse archaeological records. Extractive industries such as mining, for example, include not only the sites where ore is mined but also the sites where the mined ore is crushed and processed, transportation sites, water conveyance sites, sites for the preparation of raw materials used in processing the ore, and the like.

Identifying Research Questions

The first step in assessing the information value of the archaeological remains of industrial technologies is the definition of key research questions. Technology transfer and environmental change are two examples.

Example: Technology Transfer and Innovation

Existing literature in the history of technology argues that the principal reasons for accepting or rejecting a technological transfer or innovation are the availability of capital, the size of the firm making the decision to innovate or not, availability of knowledge about the innovation, the extent to which the workforce is unionized, and the physical and sociocultural environment, especially geographical isolation. Of these, the size of the company is considered to play the most significant role in accepting or rejecting technological transfers or innovations. Small companies, for example, live too close to the margin to take risks, and the corporate culture of large companies typically prevents risk taking. Moderate-sized companies, on the other hand, being somewhere in between the two extremes, are considered to be the most innovative and willing to take the greatest risks with a new technology. Janice Wegner's (1995) study of the mining technology used between 1885 and 1915 at the Croydon gold field in Australia's North Queensland, however, found evidence to the contrary. In this case, technology transfers or innovations occurred independently of company size. Wegner's study suggests that two factors played much more important roles in bringing about technological change: (1) the ability of mining companies to acquire capital and (2) the geological and chemical characteristics of the ore body. The characteristics of the ore body, for example, especially its variability, largely determined the need to develop new or innovative methods for extracting or processing ore.

Example: Environmental Change

Environmental change is another important research domain for evaluating the information value of industrial technology sites and monuments. The environmental impacts of industrial technologies are sometimes as dramatic as large-scale natural events, such as volcanic eruptions, floods, or droughts. Comstock era logging in the Lake Tahoe Basin, for example, deforested large areas and brought about major ecological changes. Archaeological data document many of the landscape changes not evident in written accounts or other historical records. They include changes in water flow and drainage patterns caused by clear-cutting and the water engineering systems used for wood conveyance. Other changes include increased rates of sedimentation that show up in filled-in splash ponds and other archaeological sites. Cut tree stumps dating to the Comstock era provide an important source of information about the tree species composition and distribution of the forest before the Comstock discovery. Tree stumps and archaeological sites such as the burned remains of log cabins document fire events.

INDUSTRIAL SOCIAL FORMATIONS

Industrial sites, of course, often include more than the physical remains of industrial technologies and workplaces. They also might include the material expression of industrial social formations. Typical examples of industrial social formations include domestic households, local settlements or neighborhoods, and regional settlement systems.

Domestic Households

The remains of domestic households, social groups living in the same building or compound, are commonly found at industrial sites. Industrial households include such varieties as boardinghouses, families, unrelated people living together for mutual aid, and commercial households such as brothels. The archaeological remains of industrial households include building foundations, yards, fences, trash dumps, wells, privies, footpaths and roads, and the like. Some data on household demography, including size and age and sex composition, might be contained within the archaeological record. Archaeological data that might be related to household size include the floor area of house sites and room additions. For this reason, house sites, especially those with well-defined foundations or evidence of rebuilding, are important. Archaeological remains of domiciles and domestic refuse offer glimpses into the everyday life, such as domestic consumption, domestic architecture, and foodways, of industrial workers and managers that are not available from written accounts and other sources. Archaeological remains, written records, and oral histories, for example, can be combined to interpret living conditions at different time periods. Animal remains, plant remains, soil chemistry profiles such as lead content, and other archaeological data on nutrition, sanitation, and health can be combined with documentary and ethnographic accounts of not only what was eaten but also what workers thought about diet and health conditions generally (e.g., Beaudry and Mrozowski 1988; Shackel 1996). Pollen, phytoliths, and macrofossils surviving in the archaeological record can be used to reconstruct vegetation in the back lots of boardinghouses and other workers' housing.

It should be remembered, however, that the archaeological remains of a household at a single point in time are no more than "samples of the domestic cycle through which a household evolves" (Hardesty 1992: 182). Household organization and membership, for example, often changes over time, reflecting such things as reproduction, labor demands, and the addition of boarders or domestic servants. Such variability and change in the organization of miner's domestic households reflect historical circumstances and adaptation to local, regional, and global environments.

Local Settlements and Neighborhoods

Some industrial households are geographically isolated, but most are likely to be clustered into localized settlements. Such settlements include temporary work camps, industrial towns, and neighborhoods or satellites of towns. They may occur in the midst of industrial technologies or miles away. Many settlements and neighborhoods are defined by cultural identity, such as ethnicity or nationality or gender. Most industrial social formations, for example, have places known locally as Chinatown, Greektown, or Little

Rome. Not all industrial neighborhoods, however, are defined by cultural identity. Some are clearly economic. Richard Goddard (1999), for example, found that the settlement of Steptoe City, which lies just outside the copper company town of McGill, Nevada, is better understood as a marginal neighborhood of McGill than as a separate satellite settlement or as a Mormon neighborhood of the same town.

Regional Settlement Systems

At another scale, archaeological remains might provide information well suited for the comparative study of regional industrial communities, such as those that often are coterminous with the mining district. The material expression of the regional community might be found in architecture and the built environment, settlement patterns, road networks, landscapes, and social and economic interaction networks. Margaret Purser (1989), for example, uses road networks effectively as a material and visible expression of community to define the changing geographical boundaries of the regional community in Paradise Valley, Nevada. The best physical image of the mining community probably is the regional settlement system. The settlement system includes not only towns but also outliers, such as villages, hamlets, and isolated residences or ranches.

Mining districts, which were organized by the miners shortly after the discovery of a significant ore body, often provide approximate boundaries of regional settlement systems associated with mining. Mining districts are political units in the sense of being an officially organized place with commonly agreed upon geographical boundaries and rules governing mining practices. They also are landscapes transformed by the activities of mining that may or may not take place within the political boundaries of the district. In most cases mining districts, if deemed historically significant, are best treated as historic districts within the National Register process.

Identifying Research Questions

As with industrial technologies, the first step toward assessing the information value of the archaeological remains of industrial social formations is the definition of key research questions.

Social and Cultural Change

Documenting and explaining how industrial social formations undergo social and cultural change is one important research domain. A. E. Rogge and his colleagues (1995), for example, studied the archaeological sites of work camps of Apache laborers helping to construct the Theodore Roosevelt Dam on the Salt River in Arizona in the first decade of the twentieth century. They found archaeological evidence of workers living in traditional wickiups and using globally distributed artifacts in traditional Apache ways. The workers, for example, punctured metal buckets and cans with nails to make strainers for brewing corn beer. They roasted ash bread on grills made with woven wire. And they ritually smashed and slashed metal wash basins and buckets with an axe or a hatchet.

Creating Cultural Identities

The archaeological record of industrial social formations might include information about how individuals used material things to create cultural identities. Leland Ferguson (1992), for example, found that both slaves and planters on antebellum plantations in the American South actively used material things as symbols of their cultural autonomy. He shows how slaves actively manipulated material things associated with architecture, foodways, and ritual to create their cultural identity.

Negotiating Class Relations

The archaeological record of industrial social formations also could contain information about how individuals negotiate social class relations. Social class is best viewed not as a static descriptive category but as a dynamic relationship among individuals and social groups competing "over the exercise of social power" (Paynter and McGuire 1991: 1). Class relations must be negotiated. Following this perspective, LouAnn Wurst and Robert Fitts (1999) argue for a locally contextualized and situational approach to the study of class relations. Individuals or groups often developed strategies of domination and resistance to be used in the negotiation of class relations.

Thus, Mary Beaudry et al. (1991) found that nineteenth-century textile mill workers living at the Boott Boardinghouse in Lowell, Massachusetts, manipulated material things as symbols of their rejec-
tion, acceptance, or modification of class ideologies. An example is
the company imposition of restrictions on the consumption of alco-
holic beverages by the workers and the archaeological evidence of
continued, if secret, use of such beverages (e.g., Bond 1989, Mrozowski et al. 1996). Illicit drinking might have played a role in the
labor movement by promoting working-class solidarity in the face
of company policy. Alternatively, secret drinking might reflect the
continuation of ethnic traditions and a preindustrial work ethic that
allowed workers the freedom to work at their own pace and time
schedule and to indulge in personal preferences. Paul Shackel
(1996) found a similar conflict over work habits (e.g., daily work
routines, off-work periods) between workers and managers at the
federal armory at Harpers Ferry in what is now West Virginia. The
armory first employed craftsmen from the American South, which
was dominated by a preindustrial work tradition. Later attempts in
the early nineteenth century by armory supervisors to impose the
industrial work routines used at the Springfield, Massachusetts,
federal armory met with enormous resistance, including strikes and
sabotage, from the Harpers Ferry workers. The armory eventually
changed to an industrial pattern by installing surveillance technologies, such as watch towers and constructed walls separating the armory from the rest of the town, so that workers could not simply
leave when they wanted to.

Glocalization

Perhaps more than anything, however, the archaeological records
of industrial social formations offer the opportunity to explore glocalization, the interplay between the local and the global. Certainly
archaeology is well equipped to document a global presence at localities in the form of globally distributed commodities and to say
something about geographical origins. But all too often we stop
there. We also need to construct models of how the global is locally
interpreted or transformed. Anthropologist Daniel Miller's (1998)
studies of Coca-Cola in Trinidad, for example, show that the ho-

mogenization of commodities so often assumed as a consequence of globalization is counteracted quite effectively by local social and cultural traditions. Our understanding of work camps would benefit from a more in-depth look at how work camps used and reinterpreted the material things of global origins, or how they used and reinterpreted the ideas and social traditions of homeland cultures. Under what conditions did local work camps accept or reject the global or institutional or the familiar? The commodities found in stores and consumed in the household offer clues about glocalization.

A good example is Neville Ritchie's (1993) study of the domestic and landscape architecture of Overseas Chinese settlements in the gold fields of southern New Zealand. He found that the buildings typically followed preexisting Western models and reflected adaptation to local environmental conditions but also retained some traditional Chinese elements. They, for example, used locally available construction materials (e.g., turf, mud bricks and puddled mud, forest trees, canvas, corrugated iron sheets, cobblestones) and places (e.g., rock shelters) and often took advantage of abandoned buildings. And they did not have the typical high culture Chinese architectural elements of upturned eaves, decorative eave brackets, tile roofing, and fretwork patterns on fascia boards. The buildings, however, often retained some elements of traditional Chinese rural architecture, such as being windowless and having hut shrines, door inscriptions, and a chopping block just outside the door (Ritchie 1993: 369). The traditional Chinese principles of *feng shui* played a role in building and landscape architecture in some cases, including the avoidance of doorways that faced one another, the avoidance of flat and unwatered places as building sites, building in places that overlooked water sources and that backed into terraces or sloping ground, building at the confluence of streams, and the avoidance of settlement patterns in straight lines (Ritchie 1993: 366).

INDUSTRIAL LANDSCAPES

Industrial activities typically create distinctive landscapes that can be treated as property types, most of which are rural historic landscapes. Rural historic landscapes are created not by intention or design but by repetition of the same human activities in the same place (McClelland et al. 1999). Industrial landscapes, then, can be defined as geographical regions that not only have been used historically for industry but also have been distinctively modified by the same activities. They reflect the cumulative history of industry-related land use practices, ecological or natural responses to industrial practices, distinctive patterns of spatial organization, and cultural traditions. The key components of industrial landscapes include landforms, buildings and structures, objects, transportation networks, boundary markers, vegetation related to land use, and small-scale elements, such as fences and claim markers.

Landforms

More than anything else, however, landforms give industrial landscapes their distinctive character. Consider, for example, mining landscapes. They are dominated by natural and often spectacular landforms, such as ravines and hills, and by human-created or cultural landforms resulting from industrial activities. Cultural landforms include (1) deposits on the natural ground surface, such as mine waste rock dumps, slag dumps, and mill tailings; (2) surface mining cuts and pits including open pit mines, mine pits, prospects, and bulldozer cuts; and (3) underground mining cuts, pits, and holes, such as shafts, platforms, dugouts, and leveled-off work surfaces that are visible on the surface. In addition, mining landscapes associated with underground mining are three-dimensional and include a created underground landscape consisting of excavated stopes, drifts, crosscuts, winzes, and the like.

Patterns of Land Use

Land use practices create industrial landscapes, and industrial technologies play a key role in patterning land use practices. Strip-mining, hydraulic mining, open pit mining, and underground mining, for example, all have distinctive landscape expressions. Mining practices organized around small-scale human- or animal- or water-powered machines, such as arrastras or horse whims, create small-scale mining landscapes. In contrast, the introduction of industrial mining technologies, such as steam engines or power shovels, dramatically increases both the scale and the magnitude of landscape changes. Yet another type of landscape transformation followed the invention of the cyanide process for milling ores in 1887. Higher recovery rates made it profitable to rework old mine waste rock dumps and mill tailings, moving them from their original locations and creating new landforms in other places.

Ecological Impacts and Responses

Industrial landscapes also reflect ecological impacts and responses to the application of mining technology and related activities. Thus the enormous fuel demands of steam engines at hoisting works and mills, along with the timber required for underground workings, deforested large areas during the nineteenth century. At the Comstock mine, for example, the demand for wood created a large logging industry that completely deforested much of the Carson Range and the Lake Tahoe Basin in the Sierra Nevada Mountains in the late nineteenth century.

Cultural Traditions

Industrial landscapes also reflect and document cultural belief. Industrial mining, for example, took place within a global economy that involved labor migration from around the world. Mining immigrants brought with them a wide variety of belief systems that transformed landscapes into their own images. Overseas Chinese miners or workers in the mining industry, for example, brought with them cultural principles of *feng shui,* stipulating the ideal relationships between people and nature. *Feng shui* practices include orienting buildings to face south, with calm water in front, placement at the confluence of streams but not at branching streams, square town plans and dwellings, and alignment of buildings on a north-south axis. However, the extent to which the principles of geomancy were applied in practice probably varied enormously and depended on local conditions and expediency.

Boundaries

Another question of definition is how the boundaries of mining landscapes are drawn. In some ways, the boundaries are easy to identify; the cultural landforms created by mining activities such as mine waste rock dumps, mill tailings, and open pits often are highly visible and point to where the lines should be drawn. Visual images or viewsheds drawn from paintings, photographs, or narrative descriptions also are useful in drawing culturally meaningful boundaries around mining landscapes. But mining landscapes often include more than just the place where the ore is mined. Outliers that should be included in mining landscapes, for example, include geographically separated places where there were other mines, mills, and settlements, and where supply operations took place. Settlement patterns, the material expression of local and regional mining communities or networks of social interaction, also help define the boundaries of mining landscapes. Settlement patterns mark the boundaries and spatial organization of communities. The settlement system includes not only mining towns but also outliers, such as villages, hamlets, and isolated residences or ranches. Road networks often help define the geographical boundaries of the regional community.

CASE STUDY: THE IRON AND STEEL RESOURCES OF PENNSYLVANIA, 1716–1945

The "Iron and Steel Resources of Pennsylvania, 1716–1945" MPS (Bomberger et al. 1991) addresses technological business, social, labor, and community history of iron and steel in Pennsylvania, the keystone in the development of the industry. Pennsylvania was the historical center of the nation's iron industry. The five historic contexts are described according to chronology in the following sections.

Ancient Technology, a Proper Time and Place, and Early Industrial Leadership, 1761–1783

The first forges were bloomeries that produced wrought iron directly from ore. By the time of the American Revolution, there were thirty blast furnaces and more than fifty forges in the southeastern part of the state. Characteristic of the iron plantation were ironmaster's house, workers' housing, charcoal storage house, office, company store, sawmill, gristmill, blacksmith shop, barn, agricultural fields, hundreds or thousands of acres of forested land, and perhaps a chapel, school, and specialized housing for miners, colliers, or others.

Adjustment, Migration, and Progress, 1784–1830

The industry expanded into new areas of the Commonwealth as new works were established. More than seventy ironworks, including furnaces, forges, and nail slitting mills, were established between 1790 and 1800. Technology, business organization, and labor didn't change much from the earlier period.

Mineral Fuel, Integration, and Soaring Production, 1831–1866

This period was driven by the new product demands of foundaries and the railroad. Major technological changes were the adoption of mineral fuel and the introduction of hot blast to smelting. Wrought and cast iron were still produced for household goods, agricultural tools, and nonagricultural equipment. The decentralization of the iron plantation gave way to concentration of facilities at canal or river towns for ease of transportation. The business structure evolved with rising levels of capitalization and growing factory scale. At the beginning of the period there were individual or partnership owners, and by the end companies (corporations) owned properties. There was also the first substantial effort at unionization.

The Rise of Big Steel, 1867–1901

This period saw profound changes in scale, products, technology, business practices, and labor. Huge steel mills dwarfed earlier mills. There were steel-making furnaces, continuous rolling, and integrated production as business management consolidated plants into large corporations. Labor unions developed in the 1870s, but the main union was smashed in the 1890s. By the 1890s, de-skilling had changed workers' bargaining position. By then, immigrants and African Americans were taking unskilled jobs as well.

Oligopoly, the Great Depression, and the Rise of Organized Labor, 1902–1945

During this period, a small group of companies dominated and competition abated with price-fixing. Workers acquiesced to company welfare practices. New Deal legislation spurred the rise of organized labor, and the United Steel Workers became influential.

Registration Requirements

Each of the five historic contexts is associated with distinctive property types that convey the significance of the time period to, or provide information about, the technology and development of the iron and steel industry. Property types range from eighteenth-century furnace stacks with less than one acre to nineteenth-century plantations with a furnace, buildings, and acres of archaeological remains, to twentieth-century iron-clad merchant iron furnaces. Table 5.1 shows the two main categories of property types: production facilities and the structures that were built to serve people.

Registration requirements specify under what circumstances property types are eligible under National Register criteria A–D. Under criterion A, there must be an association with the iron industry, such as a direct association with initial establishment, expansion, or introduction of new technologies. For example, Mount Etna Furnace in Juniata County, Pennsylvania, is directly associated with westward expansion of the iron industry, whereas Farrandsville Furnace in Clinton County, Pennsylvania, is associated with early coke experimentation. In the community planning and development area of significance, a property must represent the ironmasters' efforts to build for workers and themselves and must represent the educational, religious, residential, commercial, or agricultural functions of iron villages or plantations. A property must retain its integrity of design and feeling. Form and function must be readily apparent, even if there is partial collapse. It is not necessary to re-

Table 5.1   Iron and Steel Industry Property Types

I. Production facilities directly related to the production of iron.

iron furnace stacks or blast furnaces (surrounded by other production
  buildings)
engine houses
bridge houses
charcoal houses
stock houses
regenerative stoves
livestock barns or stables
casting sheds
bloomery forges
rolling mills
slitting mills
blacksmith shops
storage sheds
storage pits
machinery
roads
tramways
railroad tracks or beds
iron mines or iron pits
slag piles

II. Buildings and structures erected to serve workers and ironmasters

workers' housing
ironmaster's housing
schools
churches
gristmills
barns
stores
furnace office (and other commercial buildings)
outbuildings (smokehouses, springhouses, carriage sheds)

tain all or even most of the historic buildings. Buildings and structures need to retain materials and have integrity of location, but
there may be changes to the setting, because settings have been
much altered over time. It is acceptable if clear-cut woods that have
grown back or twentieth-century development now abuts an iron
plantation.

Under criterion B, an important individual must stand out, such as for management of a major iron company, invention or establishment of significant innovations in iron making, production of significant types of iron products, or leading the development of a major iron producing region. For example, Mount Vernon Furnace in Fayette County, Pennsylvania, is significant under criterion B for its association with Isaac Meason, the most notable of the western Pennsylvania ironmasters. A property must retain its integrity of association, and buildings and structures must retain integrity of design, workmanship, materials, feeling, and location.

Under criterion C, production facilities with exceptional craftsmanship, those that retain rare and in situ machinery, or those that are exceptionally well preserved or unusually configured might be eligible in the engineering area of significance. For example, the four contiguous stacks of the Lackawanna Iron and Coal Company furnaces in Lackawanna County, Pennsylvania, would be eligible under criterion C. Architectural resources, especially the vernacular architecture of ironmasters' houses, also might be eligible. A property must retain integrity of design, workmanship, and materials to be eligible. If the design is a reflection of the immediate environment, there must also be integrity of location and setting.

Under criterion D, a property must have the potential of providing important information. Categories of such information include the size and configuration of lost buildings, metallurgical advances through the study of pigs, information about furnace products, and information on technological modifications and the lives of ironmasters and workers. The study of slag deposits could provide information about manufacturing changes over time through the analysis of color and type of slag, which denotes the type of blast and type of ore used. The type and quality of products often can be found archaeologically. To trace the expansion or contraction of iron plantations, one might map out changes in the scale and layout of workers' housing, the plantation, and the remains of tramways, roads, and railroads. Belowground household remains could shed light on workers' daily lives, standard of living, health, clothing, purchasing or trade patterns, and family structure. Properties must retain integrity of association, location, design, and materials, to be eligible under criterion D.

CASE STUDY: WOOD'S GRISTMILL

Another example comes from the site of Wood's Gristmill at Fort Drum in northern New York state (Louis Berger and Associates 1986, 1988, 1992). Sawmills and gristmills were among the oldest industries in the region. Sawmills are extractive and associated with initial settlement. Gristmills were market-oriented and flourished with growing populations. "An important research question posed for grist mills pertains to changing market orientations of the 19th century agricultural economy and associated technological changes in the grist milling industry in northern New York" (Louis Berger and Associates 1986: 3–32). The ruins of the mill structure and the dam and tailrace structures compose the Wood's Gristmill site in Jefferson County. The gristmill ruin is one of the few known sites in Fort Drum where standing walls are preserved. These structural remains allow for ready interpretation of the mill. While there are some other visible foundations to structures in the village, they were not recorded or evaluated because the area was known to contain much live ordnance, which prevented detailed study beyond the mill site (Guldenzopf 1993).

Cereal crops and surpluses of wheat and flour exported through regional markets were an important source of cash in the diversified agricultural economy. As grain production increased in the Midwest in the late nineteenth century, northern New York mills appear to have changed their orientation to processing feed and flour for local farmers and local markets. Northern New York grain production couldn't compete with Midwestern production and lost its status as a regional grain exporter in the late nineteenth century. Therefore, there shouldn't have been any major expansion or upgrading of mills during that period. To test the validity of this interpretation, research needs to be done at several gristmills in the area. In some cases, therefore, so-called redundant resources might be necessary to address some research questions. In this case, research would focus on technology at each site, size of the labor force, and variable participation in local and regional markets. To contribute to this research, the archaeological remains of the mills need to include the entire complex, including the mill itself and technological features associated with the power source (e.g., the dam, millrace, gate structures, and machinery). Historical documentation regarding ownership, labor force, production records, and market relations must be available to substantiate on-the-ground research.

6

Domestic Sites and Farmsteads

Domestic archaeological sites include remains of residential occupations, such as dwellings and associated well, privy, garden, midden, and sheet refuse deposits. Categories of property types include urban residential sites, rural village and hamlet occupations, and rural farmsteads. Farmsteads include a variety of barns, outbuildings, and agrarian landscape features as well as house sites. In many cases, the distinction between domestic sites and commercial or industrial sites is blurred, as one examines market-oriented farms or villages that have grown up around such industries as the local gristmill.

The concept of feature system emphasizes the need to understand the whole system in order to understand smaller pieces of it that may seem insignificant. Domestic sites are parts of feature systems that include industrial and other labor, military installations, churches, schools, and other institutions, commercial sites and districts, and transportation networks. If domestic sites are evaluated outside of their social and economic contexts, then connections within local and regional settlement systems might be overlooked and their research value diminished.

It is the "series of farmsteads and rural townsites that demonstrate the diachronic and synchronic evolution and development of rural America" (Scott 1990: 52). In evaluating the complex feature systems of U.S. life in the late nineteenth and twentieth centuries, all component sites must be considered. Steven Smith (1994: 96) refers to the management challenge at Fort Leonard Wood in Missouri of the "ubiquitous homesteads of American farmer or rancher" and comments, "But to neglect them because they are so prevalent or so much less exotic is to neglect a major portion of the cultural history of this nation. As late as 1920 one in three Americans lived on farms. For most Americans, our cultural roots are tied to the world of the family farm." Smith used a combined cultural, historical, and landscape approach to develop a regional context, which assists in identifying sites that best represent the range and variety of culture history. Site types were the keys to integrating the historic context and the archaeological remains.

Researchers working on domestic sites in many contexts might address common issues such as consumer behavior patterns or modernization as well as any issue affecting people's everyday lives. Economic strategies of African Americans after the Civil War have been examined in the rural South (e.g., Orser 1990a, 1990b) and in urban areas of the mid-Atlantic (e.g., Mullins 1996). Diana Wall (1994) studied middle-class domestic sites in New York City to examine gender and class relations during the Victorian era. Issues of workers' responses on the domestic front to the sweeping changes of the factory system have been investigated in both northern and southern settings in Lowell, Massachusetts (Beaudry and Mrozowski 1988) and in Harpers Ferry, West Virginia (Shackel 1996).

Archaeology is a uniquely useful research tool for investigating details of consumer behavior (LeeDecker 1994; Klein 1991). Archaeological information provides specific household data that refine the broader community data found in newspaper advertisements, merchant daybooks, and commercial documents. The household is a primary unit of analysis because it serves as the unit of economic consumption and production. Depending on the scale of both the documentary and the archaeological data available, the neighborhood also might serve useful for the analysis of consumer behavior. With very few exceptions, documentary evidence cannot reveal actual consumer use of goods (LeeDecker 1994).

The twentieth century has witnessed massive culture change. Twentieth-century rural sites provide a data set against which to examine those changes, particularly the social change from folk to modern culture. Melanie Cabak and Mary Inkrot (1997: 17) write, "the modernization model . . . possesses the potential to provide insight into the interpretive interface between regional adoption of new technology and crop regimes, the organization of class structure and gender roles at the community and household levels, and the general way that material culture change has transpired over the last 100 years in rural settings." The mass production of consumer goods presents a difficult challenge for the archaeologist attempting to study consumer choice through subtle variations in the material record (Little 1997).

David Grettler et al. (1996) use three general research themes to examine a series of three marginal farms occupied from 1765–1822, 1850–89, and 1822–1937 in Kent County, Delaware. These themes are

- agricultural tenancy in central Delaware;
- social and economic changes of urbanization, industrialization, and the development of a powerful, volatile economy in the nineteenth century;
- the role of agriculture in the increasingly volatile economy.

The 22-acre Moore-Taylor farm, which changed hands twenty-four times, never appeared on an agricultural census because it never produced more than $100-worth of produce. The farm was constructed in 1822 during a period of prosperity when strong regional markets encouraged farm tenancy. It was abandoned in 1937 during the Depression. Trash disposal patterns showed major lifeway changes after the mid-nineteenth century with off-site disposal of trash. The analysis of five sequential wells provided household assemblages from the last two occupations and revealed evidence of a major shift in consumption patterns between the late nineteenth and early twentieth centuries from self-sufficiency to consumer culture.

Wade Catts and Jay Custer (1990) explored the Thomas Williams site in New Castle County, Delaware. The most archaeologically visible occupation was that of an African-American laborer and his family who bought the property in 1887 and lived there until 1922. This site and the few comparative sites demonstrated that there is a great variety in the assemblages of rural blacks, who, in spite of poor representation in the documentary record, participated fully in the consumer culture. One conclusion of this work is that "there are no simple correlations between patterned variability in ceramic assemblages and socio-economic status, site function, layout, ethnicity, or cultural geographic context" (Catts and Custer 1990: 266). In a very different context in urban Annapolis, Maryland, Paul Mullins (1996) finds that African Americans explicitly participated in consumer culture and used their purchasing power as a strategy to confront the racism that attempted to exclude them from American social and economic life. Such findings challenge the frequent assumption that race or ethnicity provides a predictable pattern of material culture ownership.

CASE STUDY: RURAL RESOURCES OF LEON COUNTY, FLORIDA

The "Rural Resources of Leon County, Florida, 1821–1945" MPS (Historic Tallahassee Preservation Board and Mattick 1995) includes three contexts: (1) Antebellum and Civil War Period 1821–65; (2) Reconstruction and Diversification 1866–89; and (3) Hunting Plantations, Tenants, and Yeoman Farmers 1890–1945. Leon County was a state leader in agricultural production, and most of its residents were involved in agriculture. The MPS identifies four property types: (1) Individual Rural Residences, (2) Agricultural and Industrial Buildings, (3) Rural Religious, Educational, and Commercial Buildings, and (4) Cultural Landscapes of Leon County. Each of these includes a number of more specific property types. For example, individual rural resources comprise (1) rural residences, such as antebellum plantation houses, slave quarters, antebellum yeoman farmhouses, tenant farm cabins, late nineteenth- and early twentieth-century yeoman farmhouses, and hunting plantation main houses, and (2) domestic outbuildings, structures, and features, such as kitchens, dairies, smokehouses, privies, wells, and cemeteries.

The properties nominated under this multiple property cover document might be eligible under criterion A for their association with agricultural growth and prosperity of the county between 1821 and 1945, under criterion C as fine examples of vernacular architecture, or under criterion D for their information potential. Roberts Farm Historic and Archeological District is listed under criteria A, C, and D for agriculture, architecture, commerce, African-American ethnic heritage, and nonaboriginal historical archeology. There are sixteen contributing sites and one contributing building in this individual rural residence, occupied from 1830 to 1945. The sites include a nineteenth- to twentieth-century tenant site as well as the sites of the gin and commissary, which were places of work for slaves. Research questions under criterion D concern lifestyles and agricultural practices for white farmers and black tenant farmers. Because there has been little systematic archaeology in the past, investigation should yield insights into major aspects of the plantation system and the tenant system in middle Florida. The Robertses were yeoman farmers until they became modest planters by the 1860s. Therefore, Roberts Farm was a small slaveholding farm in contrast to larger plantations. Research should provide information on the local transition from plantation to tenant farming economy. At the state level of significance, research should provide economic contrasts to plantations elsewhere in the South, because middle Florida plantations evolved relatively late.

CASE STUDY: RURAL VILLAGES AT FORT DRUM, NEW YORK

The detailed historic archaeology context developed for the Fort Drum project in the St. Lawrence Valley lowlands region of New York focused on agriculture, the development of regional settlement patterns, intrasite organization of farmstead facilities, site transformation processes, aspects of consumer behavior, market networks, and continuity and change over time (Louis Berger and Associates 1986, 1988, 1992). The emphasis on context development for nineteenth-century domestic sites was critical to site evaluation because there were few contexts available. There had been substantial research on prehistoric sites, seventeenth- and eighteenth-century sites, and even nineteenth-century industrial, commercial, and military sites, but recent domestic sites had not received much attention. In addition, nineteenth-century domestic sites are plentiful and determining significance for common site types can be difficult. Several National Register nominations were prepared as a result of the Fort Drum project (also see Kuhn and Little 2000).

The archaeological resources of Fort Drum that need to be evaluated as contributing or noncontributing are associated with key property types linked to the historic context. Property types developed for the Fort Drum project context include industrial properties (e.g., iron furnace, foundry, planing mill, gristmill, sawmill, and dams associated with the mills), commercial properties (e.g., store, hotel, post office, tavern, and combinations of these with dwellings), crafts properties (e.g., wheelwright shop, blacksmith shop, shoe shop, many of which are combined with dwellings), religious properties (e.g., church, meeting house), education properties (e.g., school house), and domestic properties, or dwellings.

Sterlingville Archeological District

The local iron industry stimulated village formation in northern New York. One of these is the nineteenth-century village of Sterlingville in Jefferson County. The archaeological remains of the rural village define the Sterlingville Archeological District. Visible foundation remnants of domestic and commercial structures are situated in two distinct areas, separated by the central industrial area.

Historic Context

James Sterling established a blast furnace in 1837, and by 1850 he owned three iron furnaces, a gristmill, and an iron ore bed. In 1855, Sterlingville had 316 residents, a hotel, a post office, a blacksmith's shop, a Catholic church, and an iron furnace. After Sterling closed his operation in 1860, the population declined to 276 people. Iron production continued sporadically by the Jefferson Iron Company until around 1890. After that, the town continued as a railroad stop on the Rome, Watertown, and Ogdensburg Railroad line and as a service center for surrounding farms. It was occupied until 1942, when the U.S. Army obtained Sterlingville and other areas during

World War II mobilization. The army demolished all structures in Sterlingville for the construction of Fort Drum.

Integrity

Military training and construction have impacted the archaeological properties. For example, fighting positions were excavated in the front yards of each of the sites on one intersection. For the most part, however, the visible surface remains of the village attest to the integrity of the district's contributing resources. The district contains forty sites, including the visible features associated with industrial, domestic, religious, educational, and commercial structures, as well as surface concentrations of artifacts. The found apparent and representative resources are the foundations of industrial, domestic, and commercial structures. Sterlingville appears to have been laid out into three distinct areas, each with a predominant (but not exclusive) property type. Foundations and cellar holes in the north end of the village indicate a residential area. Foundations of stores, churches, a hotel and a school indicate the commercial section at the intersection of two roads. The features and artifacts of dwelling sites might reflect the socioeconomic status of the residents and their positions in the iron works. Employees occupied a hierarchical management tier. The ironmaster, his clerk, the founder, keeper, molder, filler, and gutter man were all involved directly in the operation of the furnace. Woodcutters, teamsters, colliers, blacksmiths, and other manual laborers were all necessary employees. James Sterling occupied a large Italianate house overlooking the furnace, whereas his workers generally lived in modest dwellings along the road leading to the iron works. Together, these household sites represent a substantial repository of information about domestic life and social relations in a rural village in nineteenth-century New York state.

Evaluating Significance under Criterion D

The historic context suggests several research questions for assessing the information value of the archaeological resources as contributing elements to the archaeological district. Some of these are concerned with social and economic relationships among classes of workers in rural industrial villages. For example, artifact deposits of different households might reveal patterned relationships among residents engaged in a variety of occupations. Another set of research questions inquires about variability and change in household life in the rural village. Remains of commercial properties such as general stores would include the structure (or foundations) and discarded merchandise as well as, possibly, household debris. The remains of stores might provide information on types of lot use within rural villages, whether purely commercial or mixed use. The remains of crafts, such as wheelwrighting and blacksmithing, also would provide information on the use of lots, through the analysis of both household debris and discarded tools and waste materials from craft production.

LeRaysville Archeological District

Small rural villages were centers that served the administrative, social, and religious needs of the surrounding population. These villages developed around mills, transportation hubs, such as turnpikes, canals, and railroads, and administrative services, such as post offices. LeRaysville grew up around a post office and the LeRay land office after Benjamin Brown established a sawmill on Pleasant Creek in 1802. The town was named for a French émigré, James LeRay de Chaumont, who constructed a mansion overlooking the area that would become the town and established the land office.

The LeRaysville Archeological District contains twenty-six contributing sites. The foundations of industrial, domestic, religious, craft, and commercial structures are visible along the main street of the village. Among other things, LeRaysville Archeological District has the potential to provide important information about rural village formation and spatial patterning in northern New York. Households in rural villages might exhibit different consumer behavior than rural farmsteads. There might be a distinct village lifestyle that is the result of fundamentally different economic orientations between farm and village.

CASE STUDY: HOMESTEADS

Homesteads are farmsteads that originated in legislation intended to open up public lands for settlement. The legislation granted free land parcels to settlers in exchange for their agreement to live on the land, build a house, and make agricultural improvements over a stipulated period of time. Homesteading began with the Homestead Act of 1862. The beginning of the twentieth century brought with it a renewed effort to settle public lands in the American West by means of the National Reclamation Act of 1902, the Forest Homestead Act of 1906, the Enlarged Homestead Act (Dry Farming Homestead Act) of 1909, and the Cattleman's (Stock-Raising) Homestead Act of 1916 (Brooks and Jacon 1994, Rowley 1991, Speulda 1990, Stein 1990). Such homesteading laws not only encouraged settlement in the American West but also reflected a national back-to-the-land movement to restore rural values to American life (Rowley 1991). The archaeological remains of homesteads dating from the 1860s well into the twentieth century occur widely throughout the American West as well as in other areas of the United States that were once part of the public domain. How to evaluate the scientific and scholarly significance of these sites, therefore, is an important issue. In developing a homestead context for the state of Arizona, Pat Stein (1990: 30–4) identified several research themes in the form of questions useful for evaluating the archaeological significance of such sites:

- To what extent were homesteads economically self-sufficient?
- To what extent was agriculture practiced?
- What was the role of women?
- What were the patterns of land use?
- How did the social mores of particular groups evolve in response to life on the frontier?
- What were the long-range goals, or motives, of homesteaders in staking claims in Arizona, and how successfully were these goals met? and
- What factors contributed to the success of a homestead, as measured by the conveyance of a title patent from the government to the claimant?

CASE STUDY: OZARK AND OUACHITA
RURAL HOUSEHOLDS

William Jurgelski et al. (1996) developed a management plan for late historic rural household sites in the Ozark and Ouachita National Forests in Arkansas. The household sites date between 1865 and 1945. They consist mostly of "house and outbuilding remains, cellars, wells, and landscape partitions in the form of fences or stone walls. Associated artifacts represent industrial production and the development of worldwide market networks and material distribution systems" (Jurgelski et al. 1996: 1). The authors make the point that these properties must be understood not as isolates but as elements of larger communities that included churches, mills, stores, and other public places. Each rural household site, in turn, was the center of an array of activities associated with subsistence farming, commercial farming, or another rural lifestyle (Jurgelski et al. 1996: 8).

Historic Contexts

The Ozark and Ouachita management plan begins with the definition of three historic contexts within which the significance of the archaeological remains of the rural households are to be evaluated. Rather than being periods of time, the historic contexts are organized around the origins and lifeways of three distinctly different rural lifestyles: rural agriculturalists, commercial agriculturalists, and rural nonagriculturalists. The three lifestyles often overlap one another in time.

Rural Agriculturalists

Rural agriculturalists are subsistence farmers who trace their ancestry to the first homesteaders in the region who began to arrive in the 1860s after the passage of the Homestead Act of 1862. They include Upland South farmsteaders and new immigrant farmsteaders. Upland South farmers carry a distinctive cultural tradition. They originated mostly in the immigration of Celtic peoples to the Mid-Atlantic states during the early eighteenth century and later moved into the Appalachian Mountains and southward, occupying marginal agricultural lands. Most of those leaving documentary and archaeological traces in the Ozark and Ouachita National Forests, however, patented homesteads between 1882 and 1919. The Upland South farmers as a group include several geographical, socioeconomic, and ethnic variants. New immigrants had somewhat different geographical and cultural origins. They came from outside the Upland South, either from foreign countries or from other places in the United States. Many came from cities, reflecting the processes of urban flight. Others came as sojourners to engage in land speculation.

Commercial Agriculturalists

Commercial agriculturalists mostly had the same origins as rural agriculturalists but engaged in commercial fruit growing or production. The commercial agriculturalist lifestyle included small-scale commercial farms owned and operated by individual families, large-scale plantations, and small-scale commercial farms operated by tenants.

Rural Nonagriculturalists

Rural nonagriculturalists engaged in lifeways directly related to the forest. They engaged in "hunting, herding, trapping, prospecting, small scale lumbering or railroad tie manufacturing" (Jurgelski et al. 1996: 55) and in forest management services.

Property Types

The management plan identifies several archaeological property types that are associated with the historic contexts for the Ozark and Ouachita rural household sites. They include domestic houses, outbuildings, building foundations, cellars, privies, water sources, fences, stone-lined walkways, ornamental vegetation, other structures, and mills (Jurgelski et al. 1996: 8–30). Many of the property types include subtypes. Domestic house subtypes, for example, include architectural styles, such as single pen houses, double pen houses, dogtrot houses, saddlebag houses, central hall houses, I-houses, one and one-half-story houses, nontraditional houses, pyramid roof houses, and shotgun houses. Outbuilding subtypes include barns, corncribs, smokehouses, chicken or poultry houses, and miscellaneous structures, such as a blacksmith shop and a still house. Cellar subtypes include bank stores, outside cellars, root cellars, storm cellars, fruit cellars, subfloor cellars, before hearth cellars, and full cellars. Water source subtypes include improved springs, wells, cisterns, and water control features. Other structures include dip vats, hot beds, portable mill bases, and sorghum mills.

Evaluating Significance and Integrity

The Ozark and Ouachita management plan identifies several key research themes or domains for evaluating the information content of rural household sites (Jurgelski et al. 1996: 69–71). (See table 6.1 for a list of the themes.) The plan then defines three criteria for assessing the integrity and information redundancy of the sites (Jurgelski et al. 1996: 72–4):

- How many physical features are at the site, and what are they?
- What artifacts have been found at the site, and what do they represent in terms of date range of occupation, activities, or activity groups associated with the occupation, identity of the oc-

Table 6.1　Research Topics Used to Evaluate the Information Value of Ozark and Ouachita Rural Household Sites

architectural correlates of farmsteader culture and society
material culture correlates of farmsteader culture and society
settlement pattern/spatial organization
subsistence/economic organization
community structure/social organization
land use and environmental impacts
integration with the world manufacturing economy
visibility of ethnic differences
diversity in Upland South cultural patterns
impact of literacy on lifeways and adaptations
symbolic aspects of cultural landscapes

cupants (in terms of ethnicity, place of origin, associated life-way, literacy, etc.), and socioeconomic status of the occupants?

- What documentation is available for the site? What documentary sources have been examined and what information has been derived from those sources? What sources have not been examined? What sources are known to be unavailable or destroyed (e.g., from county courthouse fires)?

7

Large-Scale Sites

Historical sites come in all sizes. Evaluating their eligibility for the National Register requires taking into consideration the geographical area that they cover. The archaeological remains of the modern world can be enormous. As we have seen, some linear sites can extend for thousands of miles, in the case of overland trails such as the Mormon Pioneer National Historic Trail or the Oregon National Historic Trail. Irrigation projects in the American West can cover hundreds of square miles. Mining districts, plantations, and even townsites can cover several square miles. The Ten Thousand Island Archeological District in Everglades National Park covers 245,321.91 acres. Large-scale archaeological remains such as these constitute a special problem category in significance assessment. Typically, such properties are evaluated as historic districts containing many sites, buildings, structures, and objects linked together by a common theme. Such elements might or might not be individually eligible for the National Register, or they might or might not contribute to the overall significance of the historic district. Large-scale archaeological remains can occur entirely within a bounded geographical area or they might be discontiguous, that is, geographically separated. Linear sites such as overland trails, railroads, and canals, for example, can exist as a series of discontiguous eligible segments separated by segments that have lost their integrity and, therefore, are not eligible. Large-scale properties, such as mining districts and irrigation projects, also often are evaluated for their significance as cultural landscapes.

PLANTATIONS AND RANCHES

The archaeological record of commercial agriculture provides one example of large-scale sites. Plantations and ranches both produce goods for commercial consumption but differ in whether plants or animals are the commodity being produced. Plantations, for example, produce such things as rice, cotton, indigo, tobacco, trees, and rubber. The case study that follows of Middleton Place Plantation in South Carolina is only one example. Ranches, in contrast, raise cattle, sheep, and the like. Ranches tend to be a Western enterprise. The Pierce Ranch in Marin County, California, for example, is a late nineteenth- to twentieth-century ranch that produced diary products and beef. The ranch is listed for its significance to American industry. There are numerous examples of plantation archaeology in the Southeast and Caribbean. Historical archaeologists have studied Southern plantations almost since the formation of the discipline and, following the pioneering work of Ascher and Fairbanks (e.g., 1971), have studied the lives of enslaved African Americans. In his introduction to a volume on the historical archaeology of Southern farms and plantations, Charles Orser (1990a, 1990b) emphasizes significant issues of Southern agricultural history that archaeology can address directly. Such issues include racism, symbolism, social relations, and cultural persistence. As the archaeology of farms and plantations gets more attention outside the South, there will come to be enough comparative data to begin to ask questions about regional differences in farm capitalization, mechanization, and rural household consumption.

The boundaries of plantations and ranches encompass first and foremost the material expression of the technology of agricultural production. They may include several square miles of agriculture-related archaeological sites, such as the remains of barns, bunkhouses, cook shacks, gristmills, irrigation ditches, line shacks, fence lines, corrals, cultivated fields, and smokehouses.

Case Study: Middleton Place Plantation

Middleton Place Plantation on the Ashley River near Charleston, South Carolina, is a good example of a large-scale site (Lewis and

Hardesty 1979). The modern history of the site of the plantation begins as part of a land grant to Jacob Wraight in 1675. John Williams acquired the property in 1729 and enlarged it into an estate of more than 1,600 acres. On his death, the estate passed to his daughter Mary, who married Henry Middleton in 1741, and thus began the plantation's Middleton family tenure. The Middleton family played a prominent role in South Carolina and in American history. Various family members, for example, were a provincial governor of South Carolina, a signer of the Declaration of Independence, a U.S. congressman and Minister to Russia, and a signer of the Ordinance of Sucession. Middleton Place Plantation raised mostly wet rice, using slave labor until the end of the Civil War. The agricultural technology included the transformation of tidal marshes along the river into rice fields as early as the 1780s. In addition, the plantation raised corn, oats, peas, beans, cotton, hay, cattle, milk cows, sheep, and hogs. Henry Middleton II also created extensive formal gardens, perhaps the earliest in the United States, and experimented with exotic plants during his tenure from the late eighteenth century until his death in 1846.

The Civil War and its aftermath brought dramatic changes to the plantation. Federal troops burned the main house, dependencies, and several other buildings in 1865. Williams Middleton began to rebuild the plantation in 1867 and continued until the plantation was abandoned as a family residence in 1880. During this period, the plantation virtually stopped agricultural production and shifted to commercial mining of phosphate deposits along the Ashley River for fertilizer and to lumbering of forests on the plantation. Little is known about what took place afterward. The Middleton family sold the plantation in 1916 to a cousin, J. J. Pringle Smith, who worked on restoring the buildings and gardens until his death in 1970. Since then, cultural tourism has been the mainstay of Middleton Place Plantation.

The archaeological resources of Middleton Place that need to be evaluated as contributing or noncontributing elements of a historic district are associated with a set of property types tied to the historic context. They include the big house and its dependencies, slave or servants' quarters, rice or cotton mills, the overseer's house, wet rice or cotton production technology (e.g., tidal marsh fields, tidal rice pond, rice mill pond), warehouses and storage barns, formal gardens and terraces, phosphate mines, sawmills, landscape elements associated with phosphate mining and lumbering, such as woodlands and phosphate deposits, cemeteries and the family tomb, twentieth-century reconstructions for cultural tourism (e.g., hay barn, garage, office, guesthouse, stable yard complex, carriage house, restaurant, gift shop, craft and exhibit buildings, servants' quarters), spring house, and roads. Many of the archaeological resources can be connected into feature systems that can be associated with specific property types.

The Middleton Place historic context suggests a couple of key research themes for assessing the information value of the archaeological resources on the plantation as contributing elements to a historic district. One theme focuses on the evolution of plantation settlement patterns, the types and arrangements of settlements on the plantation landscape, and its changes over time. Both changing land use patterns and transportation networks play key roles in the evolution of plantation settlement patterns. The shift from wet rice agriculture to commercial phosphate mining and lumbering and finally to cultural tourism, for example, would have significant consequences for settlement type, location, and arrangements. Similar consequences are expected from the shift from river transportation to overland roads. The theme includes several specific questions. Typical antebellum plantation settlement patterns, for example, include both single nucleus and multiple nuclei types, but it is unclear which, if any, of these best fits Middleton Place Plantation. In the single nucleus type, the big house, dependencies, slave or other workers' quarters, barns, and other buildings and structures are clustered in one place. They are dispersed into more than one cluster, often reflecting different activities or social statuses or cultural identities, in the multiple nuclei type. Middleton Place Plantation might have had multiple nuclei early in its history but changed to a single nucleus with the introduction of tidal rice agriculture in the 1780s.

How to best interpret the political economy of the antebellum South is another theme. Middleton Place Plantation is a microcosm of the economic and political processes that transformed the antebellum South into a rural hinterland, a world-system periphery, with few local industries and services. One interpretation sees the plantations as self-sufficient and, therefore, not capable of creating a market demand for goods and services (e.g., North 1974). Another interpretation, however, rejects the self-sufficiency argument and finds the poverty of slaves, subsistence farmers, and poor whites brought about by plantation slavery to be the real reason for the lack of economic development in the south (e.g., Genovese 1974). A plethora of research questions and hypotheses that can be tested with archaeological and documentary data from Middleton Place emanate from the competing interpretations.

Finally, the material expression of cultural identity on antebellum plantations is another research theme. Leland Ferguson (1992), for example, found that both slaves and planters on antebellum plantations in the South actively used material things as symbols of their cultural autonomy. He shows how slaves actively manipulated material things associated with architecture, foodways, and ritual to create their cultural identity.

MINING DISTRICTS

Mining districts offer another example of large-scale historical sites that may encompass several square miles of mining-related archaeological resources. The boundaries of mining districts typically have legal, political, social, technological, and environmental meaning. They often include, for example, a settlement network with patterns of social interaction that defines an effective regional community, a legal organization that regulates mining claims, and distinctive geological characteristics with metal or mineral deposits.

The Black Diamond Mines in Contra Costa County, California, were prospected for coal in the mid-1850s. Commercial coal mining began in the area in 1859 and lasted until 1907. From 1925 until 1951, the area was mined for silica. At least two hundred miles of underground access ways lead into a minimum of 1,260 acres of mined rooms. There are three main sites, each of which contains coal and sand mines as well as a townsite that was focused on a particular mine, mining company, or groups of mining companies. Tailings piles are distinctive landscape features of mining districts.

One tailings pile has been quarried and eroded down to its present seven-acre extent. Welsh mining practices were followed in the Black Diamond Mine district since most of the foremen were Welsh miners. Each of the townsites and communities within the district began and were abandoned along with the mines, and, therefore, the remains are directly associated with mining activities (Praetzel-lis 1991).

As an adaptive strategy, mining transforms landscapes into a material expression of its distinctive use of tools, labor, materials, social relations, and knowledge. In particular, archaeological studies of mining districts provide data needed for the study of appropriate technology on mining frontiers. In the Cortez mining district in central Nevada, for example, the limestone quarries and lime kilns inventoried by surface surveys document an appropriate technology developed to reduce milling costs of gold and silver ore by using locally available materials (v. Hardesty 1988). The Russell lixiviation technology installed at the 1886 Tenabo Mill used lime and sulfur to make calcium sulfide as a precipitator rather than the more expensive, if somewhat more effective, sodium sulfide.

In *The Evolution of Technology* (1988), historian George Basalla proposes that technological change, mining or otherwise, is best interpreted within the framework of Darwinian evolution. Basalla focuses on the themes of continuity, variation, selection, and cumulative change to explain technological change. Using the same general approach, Donald Hardesty (1988: 112ff) modifies an evolutionary model of adaptation first proposed by Patrick Kirch (1980) for interpreting variability and change in mining technology. The model portrays technological change as taking place in three stages. In the first stage, mining technology introduced into a newly organized mining district is poorly adapted with few variants. Rapid diversification in mining technology takes place during the second stage, reflecting experimentation and innovation in an effort to cope with the new environment. In the third stage, finally, the most successful mining technologies drive out those that are less successful, bringing out a leap to a new level or plateau of adaptation. Any subsequent environmental change, such as a shift in the global market prices of gold or other world-system relationships, instigates a new cycle of technological adaptation.

Case Study: Bullfrog Mining District

The Bullfrog district in southwestern Nevada is a typical example of a mining district (Hardesty 1988, Lingenfelter 1986). In 1904, prospector Frank "Shorty" Harris discovered rhyolite deposits with substantial silver and gold values in the Amargosa Desert of southwestern Nevada. The miners organized the Bullfrog district (named after the green rhyolite deposits) in the same month, after which several mines and mining camps emerged within a couple of years. The earlier ranching settlements of Gold Center and Beatty developed as supply centers for the mines. Rhyolite reached a population of four thousand by 1909 and emerged as the central place in the district. About twenty-five hundred people lived in the town of Pioneer in the far northern part of the district. Smaller settlements in the district included Gold Bar, Homestake, Transvaal, and Bullfrog, with populations of a several hundred or fewer. Railroads reached the district in late 1906 with the completion of the Las Vegas and Tonopah Railroad, followed by the Bullfrog Goldfield Railroad and the Tonopah and Tidewater Railroad in 1907. Shortly thereafter, miners brought water into the district from springs several miles away, and the Nevada-California Power Company supplied electricity from their hydroelectric plant near Bishop, California. Most of the silver and gold production in the district came from the Montgomery-Shoshone mine, but several other mines (e.g., the Mayflower) yielded substantial amounts. At first, miners shipped their ores by railroad to mills at Salt Lake City, but they constructed a few new mills in the Bullfrog district by 1907. The Golden Age of the Bullfrog district declined rapidly after 1909 and ended in 1911 with the closure of the Montgomery-Shoshone mine. Rhyolite's population fell to five hundred in 1910 and virtually disappeared by 1916. Mining continued in the district, however, with episodes of small booms and busts throughout the twentieth century. The mines on Bonanza Mountain just west of Rhyolite and the mines in the northeastern section of the district near the mining camp of Pioneer, for example, have been worked almost continuously up to the present. Miners also reworked the Montgomery-Shoshone mine in the 1930s and again in the 1950s and the 1970s. And the district entered another boom period in the 1990s with the development of a large open pit mine near the Rhyolite townsite before its recent closure.

The archaeological resources of the Bullfrog district that need to be evaluated as contributing or noncontributing elements are associated with several key property types linked to the historic context. They include ore extraction (e.g., large industrial underground mines, small rat-hole mines, open pit mines, exploratory prospects, and trenches), ore beneficiation (e.g., stamp mills and other ore-crushing systems, cyanide mills, flotation mills), engineered mine complexes (e.g., the Montgomery-Shoshone mine and mill), mining settlements (e.g., the towns of Rhyolite and Pioneer, the small mining camps of Gold Bar and Bullfrog, and the entrepôts of Beatty and Gold Center), infrastructure (e.g., railroads, roads, electrical power stations, water conveyance systems), and mining landscapes (e.g., large-scale industrial mining landscapes, small-scale nonindustrial mining landscapes). Mining-related archaeological resources in the district, such as mine waste rock dumps, mine shafts, ore chutes, building foundations, and railroad grades, often can be connected to feature systems that can be associated with specific property types and then evaluated for significance.

The historic context of the Bullfrog district suggests several research themes for assessing the information value of the archaeological resources as contributing elements to a historic district. Certainly the evolution of landscapes and settlement patterns, as illustrated by the previous discussion of plantations, is one research theme. A key theme for the evaluation of mining districts, however, focuses on the evolution of mining technology. Archaeological resources in the Bullfrog district, for example, not only illustrate but also contain scholarly and scientific information about variability and change in the technology used in the extraction and beneficiation of precious metal ores. One set of questions has to do with the documentation and interpretation of the mining technology during different time periods. The archaeological remains of mines without history found in the district, for example, might have the potential to answer questions about their technology and general operation. Documentary sources offer more potential for providing detailed technological information about the larger mines; however, the archaeological data should provide complementary and independent data.

ENGINEERING PROJECTS

Yet another example of large-scale historical sites comes from the archaeological remains of engineering projects, such as dams.

Case Study: Newlands Irrigation Project

A good example of a large-scale engineering project is the Truckee-Carson Project, later renamed the Newlands Project after Nevada's Senator Francis Newlands, in western Nevada (Rowley 1996; Townley 1998). The project was one of the first large-scale federal irrigation schemes to be engineered under the auspices of Reclamation Act of 1902. Three years later, the United States Reclamation Service completed Derby Diversion Dam on the Truckee River, the first of a series of dams, diversion canals, and other irrigation works to divert water from the Truckee River and the Carson River, both of which flow from the Sierra Nevada Mountains, to irrigate a large tract of land in the vicinity of Fallon, Nevada. At first the project consisted mostly of Derby Dam, the Truckee Canal for conveying water thirty-two miles from the Truckee River into the Carson River, and the Carson Diversion Dam on the Carson River for diverting water into two other large canals, from whence it could be used for farm irrigation. The system, however, proved incapable of supplying enough water during low-water years. To remedy this problem, the U.S. Reclamation Service completed the construction of Lahontan Dam and reservoir on the Carson River in 1915. Another problem, insufficient drainage of the irrigated agricultural fields, became critical by 1912 and led to a series of drainage improvements between 1920 and 1928, along with the formation of the Truckee-Carson Irrigation District, a local water users association that took over the management of the project from the U.S. Reclamation Service. The Newlands Project ultimately irrigated almost 73,000 acres of desert land and provided a source of hydroelectric power. The farmers experimented for a while with sugar beets but failed because of local outbreaks of leafhoppers that could not be controlled. They also experimented with melons and other truck garden vegetables, orchards, poultry, dairy and beef cattle, and sheep. Alfalfa production, however, ultimately proved to be their mainstay.

The archaeological remains of the Newlands Project that need to be evaluated as contributing or noncontributing elements of a historic district are associated with several property types connected to the historic context. They include water storage and diversion structures (e.g., dams, dikes, and reservoirs), water conveyance structures (e.g., main canals, lateral canals, main drains, lateral drains, tunnels, flumes), hydroelectric power plants, pumping plants, construction facilities (e.g., work camps such as Lahontan City, quarries and borrow pits, roads, communication and power structures), administrative and support facilities (e.g., headquarters, experimental farm), and landscape features (e.g., areas flooded by drainage water such as Soda Lake).

The historic context of the Newlands Project suggests several research themes for assessing the information value of the archaeological resources as contributing elements to a historic district. Again, the evolution of landscapes and settlement patterns is a key theme. Another theme is the evolution of technology as discussed under mining districts. In addition, the archaeological record of the environmental changes brought about by the Newlands Project has a particularly important research value. Changes include the increased water level of the Lake Tahoe Basin, the dramatically decreased water level of Pyramid Lake, and the transformation of the Truckee-Carson Irrigation District from cold desert into an irrigated garden.

TOWNSITES

Another example of large-scale historical sites is the townsite. Urbanism is a hallmark of the modern world, and its archaeological record includes a large number of urban places. Archaeological studies of urban places in the modern world range from small rural towns to the great cities of the world. Evaluating the archaeological significance of whole townsites within the context of cultural resource management, however, is most likely to be limited to small towns. As a social formation, for example, towns are interpreted as a local and regional community or as a satellite or a marginal neighborhood. Townsites often include neighborhoods defined by cultural identity (e.g., ethnicity) or class or occupation. The town can be usefully viewed as a community (e.g., Cusick 1995, Deagan 1983) and studied from the perspective of historical ethnography (Schuyler 1988).

Kathy Deagan's (1983) study of the sixteenth-century townsite of St. Augustine, Florida, is a good example. She used an ethnohistorical approach by first establishing a social and cultural baseline for archaeological interpretation in the well-documented eighteenth-century town. Documents, for example, showed that households in the eighteenth-century town varied by social class, wealth, occupation, and ethnicity, among other things. Social classes with distinctive cultural identities lived in many of the households. They included the Peninsulares (people who traced their ancestry to the first Spanish immigrants to the town), Criollos (people who traced their ancestry to Spaniards born in Florida), Mestizos (people who traced their ancestry to Spanish fathers and Native American women), African Americans, and Native Americans. Deagan found that the households of each social class could be distinguished archaeologically. The food remains of Peninsulares and Criollos, for example, contained much higher proportions of domestic animals, such as cattle and commercially available sea fish than did the other households, which typically had higher proportions of locally available wild animals and plants. Archaeological images of the eighteenth-century households linked to a social and cultural context could then be used to help interpret the poorly documented households of the sixteenth-century settlement of St. Augustine.

Towns can be viewed as places with specific cultural meanings. Dell Upton (1992), for example, explores city landscapes as the material expression of culture. Another example is Charleston, South Carolina. The authors in the 1999 text edited by Martha Zierden use archaeological and documentary data on a series of individual properties, including ten upper- and middle-class households, as microcosms of Charleston's changing role as a center of transatlantic culture in the eighteenth and early nineteenth centuries. In addition, Kenneth Lewis (1984) and others have viewed towns as entrepôts within political economies such as world systems. Finally, Paul Shackel (1996) and others have viewed towns as the material expression of ideology, such as the surveillance technology making up part of the federal armory town of Harpers Ferry, West Virginia.

Another example is the company town. Company towns typically are patterned by a corporate ideology. Industrial company towns provide good examples of townsites as material expressions of cultures of dominance (Hardesty 1998c). The mining camps of Appalachia and the Monongahela Valley first gave rise to company towns in the late nineteenth century (Allen 1966, Roth 1992). Mining companies built and managed the towns in such a way as to reflect and reinforce company ideologies and power (Gardner 1992: 4). Town landscapes, layout, and architecture are particularly good material expressions of company culture.

Case Study: Reipetown, Nevada

The approach taken to evaluate the archaeological significance of the townsite of Reipetown (also spelled as Reiptown or Riepetown) in eastern Nevada, is an example (Hardesty et al. 1994, see also Hardesty 1998c). Reipetown's history began as a short-lived work camp next to the site of a building stone quarry that was established in the 1890s by German immigrant Richard Reipe (or Reip) that lasted only a few years. The abandoned camp rose from the ashes in 1907 as the platted copper mining camp of Reipetown. Its new life came from the large-scale industrial mining of nearby copper deposits by the Nevada Consolidated Copper Company beginning in 1904. The mining operation employed a large immigrant workforce, coming mostly from eastern Europe, southern Europe, and Japan. Reipetown rapidly became a hotbed of cheap housing, saloons and brothels, and labor union radicalism outside the boundaries of the tightly regulated company towns of the Nevada Consolidated Copper Company. During the Prohibition era, the town gained additional notoriety for its bootleg liquor industry. Its fortunes, however, rapidly diminished in the early 1930s, brought about by the end of Prohibition and by a decline in copper prices, and much of the town's population left. Reipetown came back to life for the last time during World War II. The demand for copper as a critical war material revitalized mining in the area and created an enormous demand for housing, which the town provided. Life in Reipetown continued to be outside the bounds of the corporate culture of the company towns until its final demise when the last family left in the early 1970s. In 1990, a plan for the construction of a new mill on the abandoned townsite instigated an evaluation of the archaeological significance of the site.

The archaeological resources of the Reipetown townsite that need to be evaluated as contributing or noncontributing elements of a historic district are associated with several property types linked to the Reipetown historic context. They include workers' housing (e.g., boardinghouses, family domiciles, bunkhouses), entertainment housing (e.g., saloons, dance halls, and brothels), other commercial buildings (e.g., cafés, stores, hotels), town infrastructure (e.g., roads, water lines, sewers, telephone lines, and electrical power system), urban landscapes (e.g., yards, vacant lots, vegetation clusters), and quarrying (e.g., quarries, buildings, structures, and landscape features associated with the Reipe quarry). Reipetown covers approximately 260 acres. A pedestrian inventory of the townsite located 486 archaeological features classified into twenty-six feature types (Mehls et al. 1992). The most common feature types are building foundations and other vestiges, house pits, privy pits, unidentified depressions, unidentified pits, domestic trash concentrations, tin can concentrations, trenches, coal and cinder concentrations, commercial or professional buildings, platforms, roads, fences, cellars, septic systems, dugouts, and domestic residences, outhouses, sidewalks, and wells. Many of these archaeological resources can be linked into feature systems and associated with specific property types.

The Reipetown historic context suggests several research themes that can be used to assess the information value of the archaeological resources as contributing elements to the townsite as a historic district. In general, towns can be viewed as social formations, places, entrepôts, and as expressions of ideology. Reipetown's historic context suggests that the most important problem domains for evaluating the archaeological significance of the townsite comes from two key research themes. The townsite is associated with several distinctive social formations. First, the townsite is the material expression of the domestic households of copper workers having a variety of ethnic and other cultural identities. Second, the townsite reflects at least two different local settlements. The earliest social formation is a stone quarry workers' camp. What research questions can be asked about the camp? Next, the town is a satellite settlement of the company towns of Kimberly and Ruth. Finally, the townsite is part of a settlement network that forms a larger regional community. The copper mines and mills make up the economic center of the community. Radiating out from the mines are outlying neighborhood settlements, such as the company towns, the satellite settlements (of which Reipetown is one), dairy farms, hay farms, and isolated households. Road networks link together the center and the outliers. Beginning in the second decade of the twentieth century, the Lincoln Highway passed through the vicinity of Reipetown. More automobile traffic and tourism followed. The archaeological record of the townsite should provide significant information about how the highway impacted the position of Reipetown within the larger regional community. The site of Reipetown also can be viewed as a material expression of a culture of resistance to the corporate ideology of the Nevada Consolidated Copper Company (Hardesty 1998c). Included in the culture are such themes as violence, labor union radicalism, chaotic landscapes, idiosyncratic architecture, and the gray entertainment industries of bootleg liquor, saloons, gaming establishments, and brothels.

MILITARY PROPERTIES

Military sites include battlefields, redoubts, batteries, forts, campsites, and cantonments. Many military properties might not be particularly large. Campsites, for example, might be relatively small if they were constructed and used by a small company of soldiers. Cheat Summit Fort in Randolph County, West Virginia, covers thirty-four acres. This Union Civil War fort and camp is listed on the National Register under criteria A, C, and D in five areas of significance: military, architecture, landscape architecture, communications, and archeology/historic/nonaboriginal. Issues that can be addressed include (1) the degree of standardization within and between regiments in living quarters, uniforms, supplies, and recreation; (2) internal layout of the camp and fort, specifically the placement of kitchens, privies, and disposal areas; (3) diet, including the use of wild and local foods; and (4) changes over time in equipment and supplies as the Union Army became more organized and better equipped. Boundaries include only that part of the fort and camp that have not been significantly disturbed by strip-mining. The boundaries do not include campsites and picket stations that guarded the approach to the main camp and are scattered down Cheat Mountain. Such sites were both numerous and ephemeral and are difficult to locate (McBride 1990).

Battlefields themselves are often far more extensive than other types of military properties. Battlefields often leave little to be found archaeologically. In the last decade or so, however, there has been a concerted effort by historical archaeologists to develop methodologies that can tease new and important information out of the material left at many of these properties. Traditional survey strategies are not always effective for Civil War properties, but as remote sensing improves, there will be better documentation of such places.

Case Study: Civil War Battlefields in Tennessee

The Tennessee Historical Commission and Tennessee Division of Archaeology performed an interdisciplinary study for almost ten years to identify and record Civil War resources throughout the state. In addition to consulting primary and secondary records and Civil War authorities, researchers consulted knowledgeable relic hunters in the state. Many sites had been collected over the years and many continue to yield artifacts, including "an assortment of ferrous and non-ferrous metal projectiles, ordnances, equipage and organic materials (leather footwear, cloth fabrics, wood, "hard tack," baked foods, bone, etc.)" (Thomason and Cubbison 1999: 74). All of the sites were visited and walked over by historical archaeologists. No additional below-surface testing was done. If there were no features such as earthworks visible, assessment of integrity was based on the history of land use and information from local relic collectors. In effect, the relic hunters had performed sampling of the sites (Thomason and Cubbison 1999: 75).

Philip Thomason and Doug Cubbison wrote the MPS documentation "Historic and Historic Archaeological Resources of the American Civil War in Tennessee." The archaeological resources of Civil War properties that need to be evaluated as contributing or noncontributing are associated with key property types linked to the historic context. These property types are battlefields—small engagements, battlefields—large engagements, earthworks (entrenchment, redoubt, redan, lunette, cremaillere, or indented line, earthwork of undetermined type), other fortifications (fort, railroad guard post, stockade, blockade), encampments, military hospitals, and other military components. For each of these property types, the historic context suggests several research themes for assessing the information value of the archaeological resources as contributing elements. As more work is done at battlefields, these questions will be refined.

Battlefields—Small Engagements

Small engagements include skirmishes and strategically insignificant engagements. These generally left few archaeological remains. An example is Parker's Crossroads Battlefield, which is the site of a cavalry engagement on December 31, 1862, and covers 1,305 acres.

Battlefields—Large Engagements

Large engagements are major battles and include such places as Shiloh and Corinth. Archaeological remains on battlefields of large engagements can provide important information on such issues as troop movements, tactics, and the location and duration of events during the battle. Categories of material that are likely to be found at these battlefields are:

Military artifacts such as ammunition, bayonets, rifles, knapsacks, and canteens associated with infantry.
Military artifacts such as ammunition, artillery rounds, saddles,

tack, containers and other accouterments associated with cavalry and artillery.

Domestic artifacts carried by soldiers into battle, including clothing, eating utensils, photographs, and medicines.

Burials, including large grave sites and individual interments.

Encampment sites associated with pre- or postbattle activity, such as trash pits.

Postwar artifacts, such as reunion medals and pins associated with Confederate and Union veterans associations.

Research questions associated with the battlefields of large engagements include the following:

What were the troop movements during the engagement? At what locations on the battlefield were specific units? Do the archaeological deposits reflect the written accounts of the engagement?

Where did the most intensive fighting occur? In what areas of the battlefield is evidence of the engagement most pronounced, and is this in accordance with written documentation?

What types of ordnance were used by the two armies? What can the expended ammunition reveal about the types of arms used by the infantry, cavalry, and artillery?

What types of burials took place immediately after the engagement, and how do they differ from later reinterments?

What domestic items did soldiers carry with them and take into battle? How were these items dispersed during the engagement?

If pre- or postencampment sites are associated with the battlefield, what can these sites tell us about the everyday camp life for soldiers?

What can postwar relics associated with veteran's organizations tell us about the frequency and duration of late nineteenth- and early twentieth-century reunions and visitation?

Earthworks and Fortifications

There are several categories of earthworks. These are entrenchments, redoubts, redans, lunettes, cremailleres, or indented lines, and earthworks of undetermined type. An earthwork might be eligible under criterion C if it is a notable, intact example of a specific type with high integrity. Such an earthwork might exemplify a type of military engineering or a rarely built type of fortification. Other types of fortifications included forts, railroad guard posts, stockades, and blockades. One example is Big Hill Pond Fortification in McNairy County, Tennessee, which is an earthwork built on top of a ridge to protect the crossing of the Memphis and Charleston Railroad. Another example is the Elk River Fortification in Giles County, Tennessee, which is a redoubt and blockhouse built by the Union at the crossing of the Nashville and Decatur Railroad over the Elk River. Categories of material found at earthworks and fortifications include:

Military artifacts such as ammunition, bayonets, rifles, knapsacks, and canteens associated with infantry.
Military artifacts such as ammunition, artillery rounds, saddles, tack, containers and other accouterments associated with cavalry and artillery.
Domestic artifacts carried by soldiers into battle, including clothing, eating utensils, photographs, and medicines.
Tools and other equipment used in earthwork construction and design.

The research questions for earthworks and fortifications are largely the same and include such questions as:

What was built versus what were typical designs of the period? How did designs on paper translate into actual designs constructed under wartime conditions? How were earthworks/fortifications physically constructed? What materials were used? How were they drained?
How was artillery used in terms of numbers, platform locations, and firing directions? Where were powder magazines located, and how were they built? What earthworks/fortifications might exist that were not typical or standardized designs, and why were they built?
What were the locations and relationships of encampment sites?

Were encampments within earthworks or outside the earthwork nearby? If occupied in winter, were huts constructed, and, if so, where?

Did soldiers camp primarily within blockhouses and stockades or were campsites located outside of these fortifications? What were living conditions like in these close quarters?

What can refuse or trash pits associated with an earthwork's occupation tell us about the units stationed at the site and their everyday camp life?

Many Union fortifications in the state were occupied by African-American troops after 1863. What were the differences in everyday camp life and domestic artifacts between these and those of white troops?

Encampments

Encampments are temporary military settlements. An example is Blue Springs Encampments and Fortifications in Bradley County, Tennessee, which are associated with General William T. Sherman's army from October 1863 to April 1865. Research questions associated with encampments include:

How were troops sheltered during their occupation of the campsite? If occupied during the winter, were temporary huts built? What were their size and dimensions?

What can the refuse and trash pits and other archaeological records reveal about everyday camp life? What did soldiers consume? What were their day-to-day activities?

How does the archaeological record support or differ from written accounts of camp life?

The mortality rate in encampments was high because of various diseases. Are there burials associated with encampments? Were all remains removed to other cemeteries after the Civil War?

Under criterion A, the encampment must be of particular significance in the Civil War as the site of a long-term training camp, defensive position, or winter quarters. It also must retain integrity of setting, location, feeling, and association of its immediate sites and surrounding historic landscape features. Encampments must retain historic landscape patterns, such as cultivated fields, woodlands, and water sources. Intrusions should be minimal, and encampments must possess sufficient integrity to provide a sense of time and place from the Civil War era.

Under criterion D, the encampments must have surface or subsurface cultural or archaeological deposits that are likely to yield information important to understanding aspects of military life and encampment sites of the Civil War.

Military Hospitals

Military hospitals can be found at some military sites. An example is the Camp Trousdale site in Sumner County, Tennessee, which is a Confederate Army training camp that was used from June until November 1861. The boundaries of the camp encompass the site of the building (no longer standing) used as a hospital for the camp. In addition to military artifacts, there might be medical artifacts, such as medicine bottles and surgical instruments, domestic artifacts, such as clothing, utensils, photographs, and burials, including large gravesites and individual interments. Research questions include:

How long were military hospitals occupied? What troops received medical attention at the site, and does this correspond with the casualties noted in the written record?

What types of medical treatments were performed at these hospitals, and what can this reveal about the state of mid-nineteenth-century medicine?

Do burial sites remain that contain human remains, such as amputated limbs? What can this tell us about the associated engagement and medical practices during the Civil War?

Does the archaeological record confirm the use of a dwelling as a short-term military hospital?

8

Summary

The vast archaeological remains of the modern world, the chosen domain of historical archaeology, present a plethora of opportunities and problems to the field of cultural resource management. Perhaps first and foremost is the question of how to assess the historical significance of what often appear to be very abundant, very recent, and very large historical sites that are very well documented in written accounts or oral testimony or both. What information value could they possibly have as conveyors of a history so recent that some of us have lived it? Certainly, as we have seen in the preceding chapters, the evaluation process involves knowledge and application of legal and ethical mandates, the development of historical contexts and explanatory theories, and good fieldwork practices. The reader of this book should come away with several conclusions about historical sites that will be useful in assessing their significance.

ARCHAEOLOGY IS IMPORTANT TO THE RECENT PAST

One conclusion is that the archaeological record is important as a source of historical information about the modern world as well as the ancient world. Contributions to CRM (Cultural Resource Management) archaeology counter the argument sometimes made in state offices and federal agencies that archaeology of the recent past is important only in limited situations where documentary data are not available. Documents, after all, provide only one pathway to the past and reflect the cultural and idiosyncratic views of their creator. So does oral testimony. The archaeological record offers an alternative pathway to the past, one that has its own biases to be sure, but that is independent of the other pathways as a source of historical evidence. Archaeology also contributes important information far more broadly. An archaeology of only the poor or particular racial or ethnic groups would have no comparative perspective within U.S. society and could not contribute to a holistic understanding of U.S. life.

HISTORICAL ARCHAEOLOGY IS STILL ARCHAEOLOGY

An assessment of the significance of the archaeological remains of the modern world must not ignore their connectivity to sites of the more ancient world. We sometimes tend to consider historical sites as different from the rest of archaeology because of their documents and recent age; however, many lines of continuity exist when research questions are properly framed in comparative and cross-cultural perspectives. Among others, research questions about the interaction between global and regional or local patterns and processes of environmental change easily link together modern world archaeology with the more ancient past. In discussing the role of modern world industrial sites in documenting and interpreting global and historical patterns of environmental change, for example, Donald Hardesty (1998a) observes that

> the archaeological and other material remains of industrial islands offer a plethora of data about the impact of industrial technologies and people upon local and regional environmental histories. Documenting such impacts is an important if usually neglected role of industrial archaeology. Making industrial archaeology into a tool of environmental studies may be a critical step toward understanding contemporary environmental problems and the processes of long term environmental change. If so, we may find yet another way to overcome what Johannes Fabian (1983) calls "distancing devices" that now separate the several archaeologies into ancient, modern, and postmodern worlds.

The methodological connections with other documentary archaeologies also should be obvious. Classical archaeologists, sinologists, assyriologists, egyptologists, and other specialists in ancient civilizations often have diverse sources of information as well and, therefore, similar problems and strengths. Historical archaeology also has connections with other disciplines such as iconography, art history, and oral history, all of which use texts or oral testimony or both as sources of historical information. For further discussion of the broad range of historical archaeology, see *Text-Aided Archaeology* (Little 1992) and *Historical Archaeology: Back from the Edge* (Funari et al. 1999).

THE RECENT PAST ALSO NEEDS
GOOD RESEARCH DESIGNS

Assessing the significance of the archaeological remains of the modern world as repositories of scientific and scholarly information is no different than doing so for the archaeological remains of the ancient world; it requires the development of good research designs. The field of cultural resource management in particular challenges archaeologists to develop coherent research designs for archaeological remains of the recent past that previously had received little attention. Serious interest in the archaeology of the last century and a half has occurred relatively recently. Donald Hardesty (1988, 1990) highlights this situation by discussing the historical archaeology of mining as a microcosm of the problem of addressing poorly known resources. He cautions against the creation of trivial questions that are not connected to clearly identified research strategies. It is essential to develop a coherent framework that links historic context, research focus and strategies, and key research questions with the specifics of the archaeological record. Scale is a particularly thorny problem in the development of research designs for historical sites and often involves assessment of integrity. As James Deetz (1991) points out, asking research questions about family life or household organization is a futile exercise if house sites have been destroyed or greatly disturbed. Backing off and asking research questions at the scale of the local settlement, such as a town, or even at the scale of regional settlement patterns might be more useful in assessing site significance. The effective assessment of the significance of historical sites requires the development of regional research designs, along with regional data banks to monitor progress in reaching research goals for the region and to help in identifying information redundancy.

THERE ARE MANY PATHWAYS TO THE RECENT PAST

Clearly, one of the distinctive features of an archaeology of the modern world is how to make effective use of the interplay among multiple and independent sources of historical information. The importance of interplay among multiple sources of information has been discussed throughout this book. Either documents, oral testimonies, or archaeological records provide a pathway to the recent past, for example, that can be used to formulate hypotheses that then can be tested with one or more of the others. The value of multiple sources of information about the past is perhaps no better illustrated than with the very recent past. Consider, for example, Hardesty's (1998b) discussion of postindustrial or late twentieth-century sites from this perspective.

> First of all, it must be realized that in this age of postmodernism, where scientific research is often considered to be just another way of "telling stories" with hidden agendas, the archaeological record still provides an alternative and independent source of information for getting at "the truth" in the face of claims of forged or otherwise falsified documents and the lies of oral testimony. Stories of genocide and other atrocities continue to be tested with the archaeological remains of victims in many places around the world. The archaeological remains of MIAs from the Korean and Vietnam conflicts continue to be found. And the studies of William Rathje continue to show that the archaeological study of modern garbage paints a picture of household consumer behavior that is quite different from the images that come from documents, questionnaires, and oral interviews. And how about an archaeology of Area 51?

The practical implications for assessing significance are enormous. Perhaps the most important is the desirability of using interdisciplinary teams to evaluate the significance of the archaeological remains of the modern world that are capable of taking multiple sources of information into account. Such teams might include, for example, historians, engineers, architects, folklorists, and archaeologists. And they need to be structured so that individual members of the team do not work independently to produce separate reports but together and interactively at all stages of the research process.

INFORMATION NEEDS FOCUS

What are the key issues of integrity for modern world archaeological sites? Whether or not a site has retained focus or interpretability or readability, which is something like integrity of design, is the most important issue of integrity. The assessment of the information value of a historical site also requires linking research questions to integrity. A townsite with greatly disturbed house remains has lost integrity for purposes of answering research questions about the lifestyles of particular households but might still retain integrity for purposes of answering more general questions about the town as a whole or the settlement-system of which it was a part. Scale, then, is a critical issue of integrity.

ABUNDANT SITES ARE SIGNIFICANT

Many land managers express the opinion that recent archaeological sites are significant only if they represent poorly documented site types. However, archaeologists might find that the better a site (type?) is documented, the higher its potential for addressing methodological in addition to substantive research questions. In an article entitled, "We've Got Thousands of These? What Makes an Historic Farmstead Significant?" John Wilson (1990) suggests an approach to establishing regional contexts based on extensive local history. His example is from well-documented Surry County, New Hampshire. Population statistics, agricultural productivity statistics, occupation pattern, and occupation spans of households help him screen the types of sites that could offer the best research results from archaeology. He advocates archaeological excavation for only those sites with analytical clarity provided by single-occupation by one household over twenty years or less, or by a single family for up to sixty years. In the particular context he developed, Wilson asserts that more than 85 percent of the identified farmsteads cannot address certain kinds of research questions because occupations by many households over a longer period of time has blurred the potential of the assemblages. As Melanie Cabak and Mary Inkrot (1997: 194) point out, however, there are many ways to evaluate what determines a site's information potential. They contrast Wilson's approach with that of the Wisconsin SHPO, who judges that long-term, single occupation farmsteads are the most important for studying rural lifeways. Archaeological value, therefore, varies according to historic context and the specific research questions developed in historic context.

RECENT SITES ARE NOT ISOLATED

The final conclusion is that complexity, blurred boundaries, and large size are typical characteristics of the archaeological remains of the modern world. They cannot be easily understood as isolated archaeological sites with clearly defined geographical boundaries. Mining districts are good examples. The archaeological remains of mines, mills, and settlements within the district often are distributed almost continuously in space without significant gaps, making it impossible to apply the site concept in a meaningful way. Linking concepts such as feature system and sociotechnical system are useful. Feature systems, for example, connect together the archaeological remains of the same mining technology (e.g., a pan amalgamation mill) regardless of where they occur in space. The historic contexts and theoretical frameworks required to interpret modern world sites often need to be global in scope. World-systems theory, for example, has been used throughout this book to explain historical sites. At the same time, careful attention should be given to the interaction between the local and the global. The archaeological record of the recent past often contains commodities that have been globally distributed. Global distribution, however, does not necessarily take place without changing the meaning, function, or use of the commodity within local social and cultural systems. Clearly we need to construct good models of how global commodities are reinterpreted or transformed at specific localities.

Glossary

Amalgamation. In mining, the process of recovering free gold and silver particles with mercury.

Appropriate Technology. Low-cost and low-energy technology specifically adapted to local environmental and economic conditions.

Archaeological Context. The physical matrix (e.g., soil), provenience, and associations of archaeological remains.

Area of Significance. The National Register category, such as "archeology: historic-nonaboriginal" or "industry" associated with a property's historical significance.

Arrastra. In mining, a low-cost and usually animal-powered ore grinding machine, in which heavy rocks attached to a central pivot are rotated around a circular trench into which ore has been placed.

Beneficiation. In mining, the mechanical or chemical processes (e.g., smelting) used to concentrate the metal or mineral content of ores to increase their value.

Bloomery or Bloomery Furnace. A low-temperature furnace for heating iron ores into malleable wrought iron with virtually no carbon content.

Central Place. A geographical center of economic and political power.

Commodity. An object or idea that has exchange value in the marketplace.

Core. In world-system theory, a geographical region where wealth and power accumulate.

Cultural Resource. A building, structure, district, site, or object that is historically significant. (See, also, historic property.)

Cultural Resource Management. Preserving the past through the protection and wise use of archaeological and other historical sites.

Cyanide Process, or Cyanidation. In mining, the process of recovering gold and silver by dissolving ore in a solution of alkaline cyanide.

Entrepôt. An exchange or distribution center for commodities, such as a seaport.

Essential Goods. In world-system theory, the things that are used in everyday life, such as tableware, food, and clothing.

Feature. Physical remains of human activity at an archaeological site that cannot be removed, such as a privy pit or well.

Feature System. Networks or geographical clusters of archaeological features that can be linked to the same human activity, such as a technological process or a specific social organization like a household.

Feng Shui. Traditional Chinese practice of geomancy.

Focus. The extent to which an archaeological site can be linked to a specific historic property and interpreted.

Historic Context. A broad pattern of historical development or an analytical framework within which a property's importance can be understood.

Historic District. A concentration, linkage, or continuity of sites, buildings, structures, and objects that together represent an eligible entity.

Historic Property. As defined in the National Historic Preservation Act (NHPA), any "district, site, building, structure, or object included in or eligible for inclusion on the National Register, including artifacts, records, and material remains related to such a property or resource."

Historical Archaeology. The document-aided archaeological study of the modern world.

Historical Ethnography. Descriptive and interpretive study of a culture that existed in the past using documents, oral testimony, and/or archaeology.

Historical Ethnology. Comparative and cross-cultural study of cultures that existed in the past.

Industrial Archaeology. The study of the physical remains of past industrial activities through archaeology, documents, and/or oral testimony.

Integrity, Archaeological. The extent to which the archaeological remains of a building, structure, or object retains its original design or pattern, historical association, or value as a repository of scientific or scholarly information.

Junking. Urban practice of collecting and selling glass bottles, rags, paper, tin, and other discarded items found in trash cans or dumps.

Landscape. Regions with physical characteristics that convey their distinctive history of land use.

Middle Range Explanation. Theories or interpretation that connect specific human activities to their archaeological context.

Mitigation. Management methods use to conserve the historical values of archaeological sites.

Mode of Production. As defined by Eric Wolf (1982: 75), "a specific historically occurring set of social relations through which labor is deployed to wrest energy from Nature by means of tools, skills, organization, and knowledge."

Modern World. The period of time beginning about 1450 A.D. and continuing into the twentieth century, marked by the emergence of capitalistic economies, industrialism, urbanism, and globalization.

Multiple Property Submissions. A cover document that requires discussions of at least one historic context and property types. Acceptance of the multiple property document by the SHPO and/or Keeper of the National Register means that the property types in the geographic area covered by the multiple property document will be evaluated using the registration requirements defined in the multiple property document.

Periphery. In world-system theory, a geographical region that is economically and politically marginalized through the extraction of raw materials and the availability of cheap labor.

Property Type. A grouping of historic properties defined by common physical and associative attributes.

Rat-Hole Mine. Small-scale mining operation that meanders along the ore body.

Redundancy, Information. The extent to which archaeological data at a particular site duplicates data already available in another previously documented archaeological site, written accounts, or oral testimony.

Research Design. A strategic plan for conducting archaeological research. The plan identifies the explanatory framework within which questioning takes place, the research questions that are important within that framework, the data requirements of the important research questions, and the methods to be used to gather the data.

Significance, Archaeological. The historical value of archaeological remains primarily based on National Register criteria.

Sociotechnical System. As defined by Brian Pfaffenberger (1992: 497), "the distinctive technological activity that stems from the linkage of techniques and material culture to the social coordination of labor."

Traditional Cultural Property. A property that is associated with cultural practices or beliefs of a living community that (1) are rooted in that community's history, and (2) are important in maintaining the continuing cultural identity of the community.

Undertaking. Governmental agency activity or authorization under the provisions of the NHPA.

Viewshed. A landscape with geographical boundaries defined by what can be seen or viewed from one place.

Visibility. The relative abundance and ease of discovery of material things at an archaeological site.

World System. A large-scale social system characterized by economic and political integration, economic specialization, division into wealthy and marginal areas, and social and cultural diversity.

References

Abu-Lughod, Janet
　1989　*Before European Hegemony: The World System A.D. 1250–1350.* Oxford University Press, New York.

Adams, Robert MaC.
　1996　*Paths of Fire.* Princeton University Press, Princeton, New Jersey.

Allen, James B.
　1966　*The Company Town in the American West.* University of Oklahoma Press, Norman.

Amin, Samir
　1980　The Class Structure of the Contemporary Imperialist System. *Monthly Review* 31: 9–26.

Ascher, Robert, and Charles H. Fairbanks
　1971　Excavation of a Slave Cabin: Georgia, U.S.A. *Historical Archaeology* 5: 3–17.

Bancroft, Hubert H.
　1889　*History of the Life of Simeon Wenban.* Chronicles of the Kings. The History Company, San Francisco.

Barker, Philip
　1993　*Techniques of Archaeological Excavation, 3rd Edition.* Batsford, London.

Basalla, George
　1988　*The Evolution of Technology.* Cambridge University Press, Cambridge.

Battison, Edwin A.
　1966　Eli Whitney and the Milling Machine. *Smithsonian Journal of History* 1: 9–34.

Beaudry, Mary
　1989　The Lowell Boott Mills Complex and Its Housing: Material Expression of a Corporate Ideology. *Historical Archaeology* 23(1): 19–32.

Beaudry, Mary, and Steven Mrozowski
　1988　The Archaeology of Work and Home Life in Lowell, Massachusetts: An Interdisciplinary Study of the Boott Cotton Mills Corporation. *IA Journal of the Society for Industrial Archaeology* 19(2): 1–22.

Beaudry, Mary C., Lauren J. Cook, and Stephen A. Mrozowski
  1991 Artifacts and Active Voices: Material Culture as Social Discourse. In *The Archaeology of Inequality*, edited by Randall H. McGuire and Robert Paynter, pp. 150–91. Basil Blackwell, Cambridge, Massachusetts.
Beckham, Stephen Dow, and Richard Hanes
  1991 Barlow Road Inventory Project Phase I: Government Camp to the Second Sandy River Crossing. Report prepared for the Clackamas County Department of Transportation and Development, Oregon City, Oregon.
Binford, Lewis
  1983 *In Pursuit of the Past: Decoding the Archaeological Record.* Thames and Hudson, New York.
Bomberger, Bruce, William Sisson, and Diane Reed
  1991 Iron and Steel Resources of Pennsylvania, 1716–1945. Multiple Property Submission, National Register of Historic Places, National Park Service, Washington, D.C.
Bond, K. H.
  1989 Company Policy and Alcohol Use at the Boott Mill Housing, Lowell, Massachusetts. Paper presented at the 22nd Annual Conference of the Society for Historical Archaeology, Baltimore, Maryland.
Borchert, James
  1982 *Alley Life in Washington: Family, Community, Religion, and Folklife in the City, 1850–1970.* University of Illinois Press, Urbana.
Brooks, Allyson, and Steph Jacon
  1994 Homesteading and Agricultural Development Context. South Dakota State Historical Preservation Center, Vermillion, South Dakota.
Byrd, David S.
  1992 Roads and Trails on the Tahoe National Forest: A Contextual History, 1840–1940. Cultural Resource Report Number 39, Tahoe National Forest, Nevada City, California.
Cabak, Melanie A., and Mary M. Inkrot
  1997 Old Farm, New Farm: An Archaeology of Rural Modernization in the Aiken Plateau, 1875–1950. Savannah River Archaeological Research Paper 9. Occasional Papers of the Savannah River Archaeological Research Program, South Carolina Institute of Archaeology and Anthropology, University of South Carolina.
Catts, Wade P., and Jay F. Custer
  1990 Tenant Farmers, Stone Masons, and Black Laborers: Final Archaeological Investigations of the Thomas Williams Site, Glasgow, New Castle County, Delaware. Delaware Department of Transportation Archaeology Series Number 82.
Clark, Anthony
  1990 *Seeing Beneath the Soil: Prospecting Methods in Archaeology.* Batsford, London.

Council, Robert B., Nicholas Honerkamp, and Elizabeth M. Will
  1992   *Industry and Technology in Antebellum Tennessee: The Archaeology of Bluff Furnace*. The University of Tennessee Press, Knoxville.
Crader, Diana C.
  1984   The Zooarchaeology of the Storehouse and the Dry Well at Monticello. *American Antiquity* 49(3): 542–58.
Crumley, Carole
  1994   Historical Ecology: A Multidimensional Ecological Orientation. In *Historical Ecology: Cultural Knowledge and Changing Landscapes*, edited by Carol L. Crumley, pp. 1–16. School of American Research Press, Santa Fe, New Mexico.
Cusick, James G.
  1995   The Importance of the Community Study Approach in Historical Archaeology, with an Example from Colonial St. Augustine. *Historical Archaeology* 29(4): 59–83.
Deagan, Kathy
  1981   Downtown Survey: The Discovery of 16th Century Saint Augustine in an Urban Area. *American Antiquity* 46(3): 626–34.
  1982   Avenues of Inquiry in Historical Archaeology. In *Advances in Archaeological Method and Theory, Volume 1*, edited by Michael Schiffer, pp. 151–78. Academic Press, New York.
  1983   *Spanish St. Augustine: The Archaeology of a Colonial Creole Community*. Academic Press, New York.
Deagan, Kathleen, and Darcie MacMahon
  1995   *Fort Mose: Colonial America's Black Fortress of Freedom*. University Press of Florida, Gainesville, and the Florida Museum of Natural History.
Deetz, James
  1977   *In Small Things Forgotten*. Anchor/Doubleday, New York.
  1988   American Historical Archaeology: Methods and Results. *Science* 239: 363–7.
  1991   Introduction. In *Historical Archaeology in Global Perspective*, edited by Lisa Falk, pp. 1–9. Smithsonian Institution Press, Washington, D.C.
  1993   *Flowerdew Hundred Plantation*. University of Virginia Press, Charlottesville.
Deetz, James F., and Edwin S. Dethlefsen
  1967   Death's Head, Cherub, Urn and Willow. *Natural History* 76(3): 29–37.
Derry, Anne, H. Ward Jandl, Carol D. Shull, Jan Thorman, and Patricia L. Parker
  1985   *Guidelines for Local Surveys: A Basis for Preservation Planning*. National Register of Historic Places, National Park Service, Washington, D.C. (revised 1985 by P. Parker).
Fabian, Johannes
  1983   *Time and the Other: How Anthropology Makes Its Object*. Columbia University Press, New York.

Fairbanks, Charles H.
  1974 The Kingsley Slave Cabins in Duval County, Florida, 1968. *Conference on Historic Sites Papers* 7: 62–93.
Ferguson, Leland
  1992 *Uncommon Ground*. Smithsonian Institution Press, Washington, D.C.
Frank, Andre G., and Barry K. Gills, eds.
  1993 *The World System: Five Hundred Years or Five Thousand?* Routledge, New York and London.
Funari, Pedro Paulo A., Martin Hall, and Sian Jones, eds.
  1999 *Historical Archaeology: Back from the Edge*. Routledge, London.
Gardner, John S., ed.
  1992 *The Company Town: Architecture and Society in the Early Industrial Age*. Oxford University Press, New York.
Garrison, James
  1975 Additional Documentation for El Tiradito (Wishing Shrine), Pima County, Arizona. Listed November 15, 1971. National Park Service, National Register of Historic Places, Washington, D.C.
Genovese, Eugene
  1974 *Roll, Jordan, Roll: The World the Slaves Made*. Random House, New York.
Goddard, Richard
  1999 *On the Edge: The Historical Ethnography of a Satellite Settlement*. Unpublished Doctoral Dissertation, University of Nevada, Reno.
Goodman, E., M. Walker, M. Pappas, C. Toulmin, and E. Crowell
  1990 Phase II and Phase III Investigations at Warner Theatre, Washington, D.C. Report prepared for the Kaemfer Company, Washington, D.C., by Engineering-Science.
Gordon, Robert, and Patrick Malone
  1994 *The Texture of Industry*. Oxford University Press, New York.
Grettler, David J., George L. Miller, Wade P. Catts, Keith Doms, Mara Guttman, Karen Iplenski, Angela Hoseth, Jay Hodny, and Jay F. Custer
  1996 Marginal Farms on the Edge of Town: Final Archaeological Investigations at the Moore-Taylor, Benjamin Wynn (Lewis-E), and Wilson-Lewis Farmsteads, State Route 1 Corridor, Kent County, Delaware. Report prepared for Delaware Department of Transportation Archaeology Series No. 124, Dover.
Griffin, John W.
  1994 Missions and Mills. In *Pioneers in Historical Archaeology; Breaking New Ground*, edited by Stanley South, pp 67–77. Plenum Press, New York.
Guldenzopf, David
  1993 Wood's Grist Mill, Jefferson County, New York. National Register Documentation. National Park Service, National Register of Historic Places, Washington, D.C.
Hall, Thomas
  1989 *Social Change in the Southwest, 1350–1880*. University Press of Kansas, Lawrence.

Hardesty, Donald L.

1988 *The Archaeology of Mining and Miners: A View from the Silver State.* Society for Historical Archaeology, Special Publication Number 6. Ann Arbor, Michigan.

1990 Evaluating Site Significance in Historical Mining Districts. *Historical Archaeology* 24(2): 42–51.

1992 The Miner's Domestic Household: Perspectives from the American West. In *Sozialgeschichte des Bergbaus im 19. Um 20. Jahrhundret (Toward a Social History of Mining in the 19th and 20th Centuries)*, edited by Klaus Tenfelde, pp. 180–96, Verlag C. H. Beck, Munich.

1995 Research Questions and Important Information. *CRM* 18(6): 4–8.

1997 *Archaeology of the Donner Party.* University of Nevada Press, Reno.

1998a Industrial Archaeology and the Environment. Paper presented at the Annual Conference of the Society for American Archaeology, Seattle, Washington.

1998b Postindustrial Archaeology. Paper presented at the annual meeting of the American Cultural Resources Association, Denver, Colorado.

1998c Power and the Industrial Mining Community in the American West. In *Social Approaches to an Industrial Past: The Archaeology and Anthropology of Mining*, edited by A. Bernard Knapp, Vincent Piggot, and Eugenia Herbert, pp. 81–96. Routledge, London.

1999a The Information Value of National Historic Trails. Symposium on National Historic Trails, National Park Service, Santa Fe, New Mexico.

1999b Treasure Hill and the Archaeology of Shermantown. *CRM* 21(7): 53–6.

Hardesty, Donald L., Steven F. Mehls, Edward J. Stoner, and Monique E. Kimball

1994 Riepetown: A Data Recovery Report for the Historic Townsite of Riepetown, White Pine County, Nevada. Report prepared for Magma Copper Company by Western Cultural Resource Management, Sparks, Nevada.

Hardesty, Donald L., Marion Salter, and Timothy Scarlett

1997 Henness Pass Road Inventory. Report prepared for the Sierraville Ranger District of the Tahoe National Forest, Sierraville, California.

Harris, Edward

1989 *Principles of Archaeological Stratigraphy, Second Edition.* Academic Press, New York.

Hegner, Frank C.

1994 Riverside Cemetery, Adams County, Colorado. National Register Documentation, National Park Service, National Register of Historic Places, Washington, D.C.

Henry, Susan

1986 A Chicken in Every Pot: The Urban Subsistence Pattern in Turn-of-the-Century Phoenix, Arizona. In *Living in Cities: Current Research in*

Urban Archaeology, edited by Edward Staski, pp. 65–74. Special Publication Number 5, Society for Historical Archaeology, Ann Arbor, Michigan.

Historic Tallahassee Preservation Board and Barbara E. Mattick
  1994 Rural Resources of Leon County, Florida, 1821–1945. Multiple Property Submission, National Register of Historic Places, National Park Service, Washington, D.C.

Horn, Jonathon C.
  1994 Johnson Ranch and Burtis Hotel Sites, Yuba County, California. National Register Documentation, National Park Service, National Register of Historic Places, Washington, D.C.

Hughes, Thomas
  1983 *Networks of Power*. The Johns Hopkins University Press, Baltimore, Maryland.

Jurgelski, William M., Kathleen H. Cande, and George Sabo III
  1996 *Farms in the Forests: A Study of Late Historic Domestic Sites on the Ozark and Ouachita National Forests, Arkansas*. Arkansas Archeological Survey Project 958 Final Report, Fayetteville, Arkansas.

Kammer, David
  1995 Nomination for El Cerro Tome Site, Valencia County, New Mexico. Listed July 9, 1996. National Park Service, National Register of Historic Places, Washington, D.C.

King, Thomas F.
  1998 *Cultural Resource Laws and Practice: An Introductory Guide*. AltaMira Press, Walnut Creek, California.

Kirch, Patrick
  1980 The Archaeological Study of Adaptation. In *Archaeological Method and Theory, Volume 3*, edited by Michael Schiffer, pp. 101–56. Academic Press, New York.
  1992 *The Archaeology of History. Volume 2 of Anahulu: The Anthropology of History in the Kingdom of Hawaii*, edited by Patrick Kirch and Marshall Sahlins. University of Chicago Press.
  1997 Microcosmic Histories: Island Perspectives on "Global Change." *American Anthropologist* 99(1): 30–42.

Klein, Terry H.
  1991 Nineteenth-Century Ceramics and Models of Consumer Behavior. *Historical Archaeology* 25(2): 77–91.

Kryder-Reid, Elizabeth
  1990 *Landscape as Myth: The Contextual Archaeology of an Annapolis Landscape*. Ph.D. Dissertation, Brown University. University Microfilms, Ann Arbor.

Kuhn, Robert D., and Barbara J. Little
  2000 The Evaluation of Nineteenth- and Twentieth-Century Domestic Archaeological Sites. In *Nineteenth-Century Archaeology in New York State*, edited by John Hart, pp. 1–16. New York State Museum, Albany.

LeeDecker, Charles H.
  1994 Discard Behavior on Domestic Historic Sites: Evaluation of Contexts for the Interpretation of Household Consumption Patterns. *Journal of Archaeological Method and Theory* 1(4): 345–75.

Leone, Mark
  1988 The Relationship between Archaeological Data and the Documentary Record: 18th Century Gardens in Annapolis, Maryland. *Historical Archaeology* 22: 29–35.
  1984 Interpreting Ideology in Historical Archaeology. In *Ideology, Power, and Prehistory,* edited by Daniel Miller and Christopher Tilly, pp. 25–36. Cambridge University Press, Cambridge.

Leone, Mark P., and Parker B. Potter Jr., eds.
  1988 *The Recovery of Meaning: Historical Archaeology in the Eastern United States.* Smithsonian Institution Press, Washington, D.C.

Leone, Mark P., and Paul A. Shackel
  1988 Plane and Solid Geometry in Colonial Gardens in Annapolis, Maryland. In *Earth Patterns: Essays in Landscape Archaeology,* edited by William Kelso and Rachel Most, pp. 153–68. University Press of Virginia, Charlottesville.

Lewis, Kenneth E.
  1984 *The American Frontier: An Archaeological Study of Settlement Pattern and Process.* Academic Press, New York.

Lewis, Kenneth E., and Donald L. Hardesty
  1979 *Middleton Place: Initial Archeological Investigations at an Ashley River Rice Plantation.* Research Manuscript Series Number 148, Institute of Archeology and Anthropology, University of South Carolina, Columbia.

Lindstrom, Susan G., and Jeffrey T. Hall
  1994 Cultural Resources Inventory and Evaluation Report for the Proposed Spooner Summit and East Shore Project (Big Gulp) Timber Sales. Report prepared for Carson Ranger District, Toiyabe National Forest and Lake Tahoe Basin Management Unit. BioSystems Analysis, Santa Cruz, California.

Lingenfelter, Richard
  1986 *Death Valley and the Amargosa.* University of California Press, Berkeley.

Lipe, William
  1974 A Conservation Model for American Archaeology. *The Kiva* 39: 213–45.
  1984 Value and Meaning in Cultural Resources. In *Approaches to the Archaeological Heritage,* edited by Henry Cleere, pp. 1–11. Cambridge University Press, Cambridge.

Little, Barbara J.
  1994a People with History: An Update on Historical Archaeology in the United States. *Journal of Archaeological Method and Theory* 1(1): 5–40.

1994b 'She Was . . . an Example to Her Sex,' Possibilities for a Feminist Historical Archaeology. In *Historical Archaeology of the Chesapeake,* edited by Paul A. Shackel and Barbara J. Little, pp. 189–204. Smithsonian Institution Press, Washington, D.C.

1997   Expressing Ideology without a Voice, or, Obfuscation and the Enlightenment. *International Journal of Historical Archaeology* 1(3): 225–41.

1998   Cultural Landscapes of Printers and the "heav'n-taught art" in Annapolis, Maryland. In *Annapolis's Pasts: Contributions from Archaeology in Annapolis,* edited by P. A. Shackel, P. R. Mullins, and M. S. Warner, pp. 225–43. University of Tennessee Press, Knoxville.

1999   Nominating Archaeological Sites to the National Register of Historic Places: What's the Point? *SAA Bulletin* 17(4): 19.

Little, Barbara J., Jan Townsend, Erika Martin Seibert, John Sprinkle, and John Knoerl

2000   *Guidelines for Evaluating and Registering Archeological Properties.* National Register of Historic Places, National Park Service, Washington, D.C.

Little, Barbara J., ed.

1992   *Text-Aided Archaeology.* CRC Press, Boca Raton, Florida.

Louis Berger and Associates

1986   Re-evaluation of Rural Historic Contexts for the Fort Drum, New York, Vicinity. The Cultural Resource Group, Louis Berger and Associates, East Orange, New Jersey.

1988   A Report on the Rural Village and Iron Industry Historic Contexts of the Fort Drum, New York, Vicinity. The Cultural Resource Group, Louis Berger and Associates, East Orange, New Jersey.

1992   The Cultural Resources of Fort Drum, Introduction to the Program and Synthesis of Principal Findings. The Fort Drum Cultural Resource Project Task Order 17. Louis Berger and Associates, East Orange, New Jersey.

Lowenthal, David

1985   *The Past Is a Foreign Country.* Cambridge University Press, Cambridge.

McBride, Kim

1990   Cheat Summit Fort, Randolph County, West Virginia. National Register Documentation. National Park Service, National Register of Historic Places, Washington, D.C.

McClelland, Linda Flint, J. Timothy Keller, Genevieve P. Keller, and Robert Z. Melnick

1999   *Guidelines for Evaluating and Documenting Rural Historic Landscapes. National Register Bulletin* originally issued 1989, revised 1999.

McDonald, J. D., L. J. Zimmerman, A. L. McDonald, W. Tall Bull, and T. Rising Sun

1991   The Northern Cheyenne Outbreak of 1879: Using Oral History and Archaeology as Tools of Resistance. In *The Archaeology of Inequality,* edited by Randall H. McGuire and Robert Paynter, pp. 64–78. Basil Blackwell, Oxford.

McGimsey, Charles R.
1972   *Public Archeology*. Seminar Press, New York.

Mehls, Steven F., Donald L. Hardesty, Thomas J. Lennon, and Robert Peterson
1992   A Class III Cultural Resources Inventory of the Historic Townsite of Riepetown, White Pine County, Nevada. Report BLM CRR-04-1055(P), on File at the Bureau of Land Management, Ely District Office, Ely, Nevada.

Miller, Daniel
1998   Coca Cola: A Black Sweet Drink from Trinidad. In *Material Cultures*, edited by Daniel Miller, pp. 169–87. University of Chicago Press, Chicago.

Moore, Wilbert E.
1965   *The Impact of Industry*. Prentice-Hall, Englewood Cliffs, New Jersey.

Mrozowski, Stephen A., Grace H. Zeising, and Mary C. Beaudry
1996   *Living on the Boott: Historical Archaeology at the Boott Mills Boardinghouses, Lowell, Massachusetts*. University of Massachusetts Press, Amherst.

Mullins, Paul R.
1996   The Contradictions of Consumption: An Archaeology of African America and Consumer Culture, 1850–1930. Ph.D. Dissertation, University of Massachusetts, Amherst.

National Park Service
1991a   *How to Complete the National Register Registration Form. National Register Bulletin* 16A. National Park Service, National Register of Historic Places, Washington, D.C.

1991b   *How to Complete the Multiple Property Documentation Form. National Register Bulletin* 16B. National Park Service, National Register of Historic Places, Washington, D.C.

1991c   *How to Apply the National Register Criteria for Evaluation. National Register Bulletin* 15. National Park Service, National Register of Historic Places, Washington, D.C.

1996   *Revised Thematic Framework*. National Park Service, Washington, D.C.

Noble, Bruce, and Robert Spude
1992   *Guidelines for Identifying, Evaluating, and Registering Historic Mining Properties. National Register Bulletin* 42. National Park Service, National Register of Historic Places, Washington, D.C.

Noel Hume, Ivor
1982   *Martin's Hundred*. Knopf, New York.

North, Douglas
1974   *Growth and Welfare in the American Past: A New Economic History*. Prentice-Hall, Englewood Cliffs, New Jersey.

Nowak, Timothy
1993   Workin' on the Railroad: An Examination of 19th Century Resources Associated with the Union Pacific Railroad through Wyoming. Paper

presented at the Annual Conference of the Society for Historical Archaeology, Kansas City, Missouri.

Orser, Charles E. Jr.

1988   The Archaeological Analysis of Plantation Society: Replacing Status and Caste with Economics and Power. *American Antiquity* 53(4): 735–51.

1990a   *Historical Archaeology on Southern Plantations and Farms*. Thematic Issue edited by Charles Orser Jr. *Historical Archaeology* 24(4).

1990b   Historical Archaeology on Southern Plantations and Farms: Introduction. *Historical Archaeology* 24(4): 1–6.

Orser, Charles Jr., and Brian Fagan

1995   *Historical Archaeology*. HarperCollins, New York.

Otto, John

1984   *Cannon's Point Plantation, 1794–1860: Living Conditions and Status Patterns in the Old South*. Academic Press, New York.

Palmer, Marilyn, and Peter Neaverson

1998   *Industrial Archaeology*. Routledge, London.

Parker, Patricia, and Thomas F. King

1998   *Guidelines for Evaluating and Documenting Traditional Cultural Properties. National Register Bulletin* 38. National Park Service, National Register of Historic Places, Washington, D.C.

Paynter, Robert, and Randall H. McGuire

1991   The Archaeology of Inequality: Material Culture, Domination, and Resistance. In *The Archaeology of Inequality*, edited by Randall H. McGuire and Robert Paynter, pp. 1–27. Basil Blackwell, Oxford.

Pfaffenberger, Brian

1992   The Social Anthropology of Technology. *Annual Review of Anthropology* 21: 491–516.

Praetzellis, Adrian

1991   Black Diamond Mines. National Register Documentation, National Park Service, National Register of Historic Places, Washington, D.C.

Praetzellis, Mary, and Adrian Praetzellis

1990   Junk! Archaeology of the Pioneer Junk Store, 1877–1908. Papers in Northern California Archaeology, Number 4. Anthropological Studies Center, Sonoma State University, Rohnert Park, California.

Purser, Margaret

1989   All Roads Lead to Winnemucca: Local Road Systems and Community Material Culture in Nineteenth-Century Nevada. In *Perspectives in Vernacular Architecture, III*, edited by Thomas Carter and Bernard Herman, pp. 120–34. University of Missouri Press, Columbia.

Rathje, William, and Cullen Murphy

1990   *Rubbish! The Archaeology of Garbage*. HarperCollins, New York.

Reitz, Elizabeth

1994   Zooarchaeological Analysis of a Free African Community: Gracia Real de Santa Teresa de Mose. *Historical Archaeology* 28(1): 23–40.

Reps, John
   1979   *A History of Frontier Urban Planning.* Princeton University Press, Princeton, New Jersey.

Ritchie, Neville
   1993   Form and Adaptation: Nineteenth Century Chinese Miners' Dwellings in Southern New Zealand. In *Hidden Heritage, Historical Archaeology of the Overseas Chinese*, edited by Priscilla Wegars, pp. 335–73. Baywood Publishing Company, Amityville, New York.

Robbins, William
   1994   *Colony and Empire.* University Press of Kansas, Lawrence.

Rogge, A. E., D. L. McWatters, M. Keane, and R. Emanuel
   1995   *Raising Arizona's Dams: Daily Life, Danger, and Discrimination in the Dam Construction Camps of Central Arizona, 1890s–1940s.* University of Arizona Press, Tucson.

Roth, Leland M.
   1992   Company Towns in the Western United States. In *The Company Town, Architecture and Society in the Early Industrial Age*, edited by John S. Garner, pp. 173–205. Oxford University Press, New York.

Rowley, William D.
   1988   *Farming Context.* State of Nevada Comprehensive Preservation Plan, edited by Ronald James and James Bernstein, State Historic Preservation Office, Carson City, Nevada.
   1994   *Reclaiming the Arid West: The Career of Francis G. Newlands.* Indiana University Press, Bloomington.

Sanderson, S. K., and Thomas D. Hall
   1995   World System Approaches to World Historical Change. In *Civilizations and World Systems: Studying World-Historical Change*, edited by S. K. Sanderson, pp. 95–108. AltaMira Press, Walnut Creek, California.

Schaafsma, Curtis F.
   1989   Significant until Proven Otherwise: Problems versus Representative Samples. In *Archaeological Heritage Management in the Modern World*, edited by Henry Cleere, pp. 38–51. Unwin Hyman, London.

Schiffer, Michael
   1987   *Formation Processes of the Archaeological Record.* University of New Mexico Press, Albuquerque.

Schuyler, Robert
   1988   Archaeological Remains, Documents, and Anthropology: A Call for a New Culture History. *Historical Archaeology* 22(1): 6–42.

Scott, Douglass D.
   1990   Site Significance and Historical Archaeology: A Scenario and Commentary. *Historical Archaeology* 24(2): 42–54.

Seasholes, Nancy S.
   1988   On the Use of Historical Maps. In *Documentary Archaeology*, edited by Mary Beaudry, pp. 92–118. Cambridge University Press, Cambridge.

Seifert, Donna J., with Barbara J. Little, Beth L. Savage, and John H. Sprinkle Jr.
   1997   Defining Boundaries for National Register Properties. National Park Service, National Register for Historic Places, Washington, D.C.
Shackel, Paul A.
   1993   Prospects for an Archeology of the People without History. In *Interdisciplinary Investigations of Domestic Life in Government Block B: Perspectives on Harpers Ferry's Armory and Commercial District*, edited by Paul A. Shackel, chapter 18. U.S. Department of the Interior, National Park Service, Harpers Ferry National Historical Park.
   1996   *Culture Change and the New Technology: An Archaeology of the Early American Industrial Era*. Plenum Press, New York.
Shackel, Paul A., and Barbara J. Little, eds.
   1994   *Historical Archaeology of the Chesapeake*. Smithsonian Institution Press, Washington, D.C.
Shackel, Paul, Paul R. Mullins, and Mark S. Warner, eds.
   1998   *Annapolis's Pasts: Contributions from Archaeology in Annapolis*. University of Tennessee Press, Knoxville.
Shapiro, Gary
   1984   A Soil Resistivity Survey of 16th-Century Puerto Real, Haiti. *Journal of Field Archaeology* 11(1): 101–10.
Smith, Duane
   1987   *Mining America*. University Press of Kansas, Lawrence.
Smith, Steven
   1994   Context and Archaeology of Settler Communities: An Example from Fort Leonard Wood, Missouri. In *Settler Communities in the West: Historic Contexts for Cultural Resource Managers of Department of Defense Lands*, edited by Robert Lyon, pp. 95–105. National Park Service, Rocky Mountain Region, Denver.
Solury, Theresa
   1999   Draft Historic Context on Labor Archaeology. National Park Service, National Register of Historic Places, Washington D.C.
South Dakota State Historic Preservation Center
   1985   *Standards for the Survey of Historic Mining and Milling Sites*. Vermillion, South Dakota.
Spencer-Wood, Suzanne
   1991   Toward an Historical Archaeology of Materialistic Domestic Reform. In *The Archaeology of Inequality*, edited by Robert Paynter and Randall McGuire, pp. 231–86. Basil Blackwell, Oxford.
Speulda, LuAnn
   1990   *Oregon Farmstead Context*. State Historic Preservation Office, Salem, Oregon.
Stein, Pat
   1990   *Homesteading in Arizona, 1862–1940: A Guide to Studying, Evaluating, and Preserving Historic Homesteads*. State Historic Preservation Office, Arizona State Parks, Tucson.

1995 Logging Railroad Resources of the Coconino and Kaibab National Forests MPS. National Register Documentation. National Park Service, National Register of Historic Places, Washington, D.C.

Supernowicz, Dana
1990 A Contextual History, Programmatic Agreement, and Evaluation Plan for Historic Water Conveyance Systems on the Eldorado National Forest, California. Eldorado National Forest, Placerville, California.

Tainter, Joseph, and G. J. Lucas
1983 Epistemology of the Significance Concept. *American Antiquity* 48: 707–19.

Thomas, David Hurst
1990 The Archaeology of Mission Santa Catalina de Guale: Our First 15 Years. In *The Missions of La Florida,* edited by Bonnie G. McEwan, pp. 1–34. University Press of Florida, Gainesville.

Thomason, Philip, and Doug Cubbison
1999 Historic and Historic Archaeological Resources of the American Civil War in Tennessee MPS. National Register Documentation. National Park Service, National Register of Historic Places, Washington, D.C.

Townley, John M.
1998 *Turn This Water into Gold, The Story of the Newlands Project,* Second Edition. Edited and additional chapters by Susan A. James. Nevada Historical Society, Reno.

Trinkley, Michael
1990 Rosemont Plantation. Laurens County, South Carolina. National Register Documentation, National Park Service, National Register of Historic Paces, Washington, D.C.

United States Department of the Interior
1983 Secretary of the Interior's Standards and Guidelines for Archeology and Historic Preservation. *Federal Register* 48(190).

Upton, Dell
1992 The City as Material Culture. In *The Art and Mystery of Historical Archaeology,* edited by Mary Beaudry and Anne Yentsch, pp. 51–74. CRC Press, Boca Raton, Florida.

Vogel, Robert C., and David G. Stanley
1991 Portage Trails in Minnesota, 1630s–1870s MPS. National Register Documentation. National Park Service, National Register of Historic Places, Washington, D.C.

Waldorf, G., G. Doran, and B. Mattick
1994 Roberts Farm District. National Register nomination (under MPS cover: Rural Resources of Leon County, Florida, 1821–1945).

Wall, Diana DiZerega
1994 *The Archaeology of Gender: Separating the Spheres in Urban America.* Plenum, New York.

Wallace, Anthony F. C.
  1972   *Rockdale, the Growth of an American Village in the Early Industrial Revolu-*
         tion. Alfred A. Knopf, New York.
Wallerstein, Immanuel
  1974   *The Modern World-System.* Academic Press, New York.
Wegner, Janice H.
  1995   *Croydon: Technology Transfer on a North Queensland Goldfield, 1885–*
         1915. Unpublished Doctoral Dissertation, James Cook University of
         North Queensland, Australia.
Weymouth, John W.
  1986   Geophysical Methods of Archaeological Site Surveying. In *Advances*
         in Archaeological Method and Theory, Volume 9, edited by Michael
         Schiffer, pp. 311–95. Academic Press, Orlando, Florida.
White, William G., Ronald M. James, and Richard Bernstein, eds.
  1991   *Nevada Comprehensive Preservation Plan.* State of Nevada, Division of
         Historic Preservation and Archaeology, Carson City.
Williams, Jack
  1992   The Archaeology of Underdevelopment and the Military Frontier of
         New Spain. *Historical Archaeology* 26(1): 7–21.
Wilson, John
  1990   We've Got Thousands of These? What Makes an Historic Farmstead
         Significant? *Historical Archaeology* 24(2): 23–33.
Wolf, Eric
  1982   *People without History.* University of California Press, Berkeley.
Worrell, John
  1985   Re-creating Ceramic Production and Tradition in a Living History
         Laboratory. In *Domestic Pottery of the Northeastern United States, 1625–*
         1850, edited by Sarah Turnbaugh, pp. 81–97. Academic Press, New
         York.
Wurst, LouAnn, and Robert K. Fitts
  1999   Introduction: Why Confront Class? *Historical Archaeology* 33(1): 1–6.
Zierden, Martha, ed.
  1999   Special Issue: Charleston in the Context of Trans-Atlantic Culture.
         Historical Archaeology 33(3).

Index

Adams, Robert MaC., 26–27
African American sites, 41, 65, 68, 74–75, 107, 120, 121–22, 123, 134, 135–36; Annapolis, 122; Cannon's Point, 65; Gracia Real de Santa Teresa de Mose, 57, 68; Monticello, 68, 56–57; Parting Ways, 68; Thomas Williams, 121–22
agricultural sites: commercial agriculturalists, 129; farmsteads, xi, 20, 71, 119–20, 123; homesteads, 127; irrigation, 141–42; plantations, 35, 56, 65, 66, 74–75, 77, 123, 134–37; ranches, 134; rural agriculturalists, 122–26, 128–29
Amin, Samir, 30
archaeometry, 101, 102
Ascher, Robert, and Charles Fairbanks, 134
Asian American sites, 5

Basalla, George, 26, 138
Battison, Edwin, 102
battlefields. *See* military sites
Beaudry, Mary, 57, 108
Beckham, Steven, and Richard Hanes, 95
boardinghouses, 108
Braudel, Fernand, 73
Brown, Marley, 66

Byrd, David, 95

Cabak, Melanie, and Mary Inkrot, 55, 120–21, 158
cemeteries and graves, 39, 40
class relations, 107–8
consumer behavior, 20, 55, 67, 94, 108–9, 120–21, 122, 123, 126, 158–59
context, archaeological, 26, 38, 53, 54, 59–60, 61, 85
context, historic. *See* historic context
contributing and noncontributing properties. *See* National Register evaluation
Crader, Diana, 56
Crumley, Carole, 28
cultural identity, 82, 107

Deagan, Kathleen, 30, 68, 143
Deetz, James, 27, 65, 66, 67, 68, 155
determination of eligibility (DOE). *See* National Register evaluation
discontinguous property, 15, 80, 86, 133
district, historic, 11, 12–13, 79, 133
Donner Party, 34, 56, 64, 68, 71

emigrant camps, 93–94
environment, 19, 28–30, 83–84, 103–4, 154

179

About the Authors

Donald L. Hardesty is professor of anthropology at the University of Nevada, Reno. A native of West Virginia, he moved to Washington, D.C., after high school, worked at the National Bureau of Standards, and attended George Washington University at night, with the intention of becoming an electrical engineer. He first became interested in archaeology during weekend visits to the Smithsonian Institution, eventually moving to the University of Kentucky (B.A.) and then to the University of Oregon (M.A., Ph.D.) to pursue academic training in archaeology. Hardesty has conducted archaeological fieldwork in the American West, the American Southeast, Mexico, and Guatemala and has been the principal investigator of more than sixty cultural resource management projects. He is the author of several books and/or monographs, including *The Archaeology of Mining and Miners* (Society for Historical Archaeology, 1988) and most recently *The Archaeology of the Donner Party* (University of Nevada Press, 1997). Hardesty is a past president of the Society for Historical Archaeology, past president of the Mining History Association, current president of the Register of Professional Archaeologists, and a long-time member of the state of Nevada Board of Museums and History, which reviews National Register nominations.

Barbara J. Little has worked for the National Park Service since 1992, first in the National Capital Region's archeology program, next as the archeologist at the National Register of Historic Places, and currently in the Archeology and Ethnography Program. She became hooked on archaeology after taking field school with Jim

Hatch at Penn State University in 1978. She worked on the Archaeology in Annapolis project, writing her dissertation on the historical archaeology of the Green Family and its printing business, partly with the help of a Smithsonian predoctoral fellowship. After receiving her Ph.D. in 1987 from the State University of New York, Buffalo, she taught (and learned a great deal from wonderful students) at both George Mason University in Fairfax, Virginia, and the University of Maryland, College Park. Her research interests include historical archaeology, theory and methodology, including feminist theory and the uses of text and documentation, archaeology and the public, and public history. She is the editor of *Text-Aided Archaeology* (CRC Press, 1992) and the coeditor of *The Historical Archaeology of the Chesapeake* (Smithsonian Institution Press, 1994).